ISBN 978-1-5279-8888-0
PIBN 10162652

MARITIME COURT, ONTARIO.

GENERAL RULES (1889)

AND

STATUTES,

WITH

FORMS, TABLE OF FEES, &c.

BY

ALFRED HOWELL,

OF OSGOODE HALL, BARRISTER-AT-LAW,

(Author of Surrogate Courts Practice, and Naturalization and Nationality in Canada.)

AND

ALEXANDER DOWNEY,

OFFICIAL REPORTER, MARITIME COURT, TORONTO.

TORONTO:

ROWSELL AND HUTCHISON.

1889.

Rowsell and Hutchison, Printers, King Street East.

ADVERTISEMENT.

The new Rules, Forms, and Table of Fees for the Maritime Court, which came into operation 1st May 1889, supersede the Rules of 1878'9, and effect almost an entire change in the practice and procedure of the Court; a change which must meet with the approval of suitors, and of the legal profession generally, based as it is, to a large extent, upon the Vice Admiralty Courts Rules, 1883, and the Rules of the Supreme Court of ~~Jurisdiction~~ Judicature, with such other modifications of the former practice as the eleven years, during which the Maritime Jurisdiction Act has been in operation, may have shown to be expedient.

The reported decisions upon the Act are, as yet, not numerous; but those that are reported, have been arranged alphabetically, with heads of subjects, and are inserted for purposes of reference. No attempt is made toward a general treatise on Admiralty or Maritime Law; that would have been much beyond the scope of the present work; and only such parts of the Statutory Law have been introduced, as are more immediately connected with the Rules, and more frequently referred to in practice. Pleadings and other Forms in common use have been appended, and the whole has been carefully indexed.

The authors entertain the hope, that practitioners, by using the present compilation, will find their labours in this comparatively new field, very greatly facilitated.

A. H.
A. D.

TORONTO, July, 1889.

CONTENTS.

THE MARITIME COURT ACT, ONTARIO.

Revised Statutes of Canada, 1886. Chapter 137.

A. D. 1886.

An Act Respecting the Maritime Court of Ontario.

HER Majesty, by and with the advice and consent of the Senate and House of Commons of Canada, enacts as follows:—

SHORT TITLE.

1. This Act may be cited as "*The Maritime Court Act*," 40 V., c. 21, s. 22. Short title.

INTERPRETATION.

2. In this Act, unless the context otherwise requires,— Interpretation.

(*a.*) The expression "the court" means the Maritime Court of Ontario; "Court."

(*b.*) The expression "judge" means the judge of the Maritime Court of Ontario; and— "Judge."

(*c.*) The expression "ship" includes every description of vessel used in navigation not propelled by oars. 45 V., c. 34, s. 5. "Ship."

COURT AND JUDGES.

3. The superior court of maritime jurisdiction now existing in the Province of Ontario, under the name of "The Maritime Court of Ontario," is hereby continued under such name, and shall continue to be a court of record. 40 V., c. 21, s. 2, *part*. Court continued.

4. The Governor in Council may appoint any judge of any superior or county court in Ontario, or any barrister in Ontario, of not less than seven years' standing, to be the judge of the court. 40 V., c. 21, s. 5. Appointment of judge.

5. The judge shall hold office during good behaviour, but shall be removable by the Governor General on address of the Senate and House of Commons. 40 V., c. 21, s. 6, *part*. Tenure of office.

6. The judge shall receive no fees, but shall receive a salary of six hundred dollars per annum, free and clear from all deductions whatsoever, and *pro rata* for any shorter time than a year, which salary shall be paid out of any unappropriated moneys forming part of the Consolidated Revenue Fund of Canada, in like manner as the salaries of other judges. 40 V., c. 21, s. 7. Remuneration.

7. The Governor in Council may, from time to time, appoint one or more judges of county courts in Ontario, or barristers of not less than seven years' standing in Ontario, to be a surrogate judge or surrogate judges of the said court: Appointment of surrogate judges.

Powers.

2. Such surrogate judge shall have such of the powers of the judge as are conferred by the commission appointing him :

Tenure of office.

3. He shall hold office during pleasure, but his appointment shall not be vacated by a vacancy in the office of the judge :

Remuneration.

4. He may, if resident elsewhere than in Toronto, receive emoluments fixed, from time to time, by the Governor in Council, raised out of funds provided by suitor's fees, payable under a tariff fixed, from time to time, by the Governor in Council :

Tariff to be laid before Parliament.

5. Copies of the tariff shall be, as soon as possible, laid before both Houses of Parliament, and entered on the records of the court, and published in the *Canada Gazette* :

Disposal of fees.

6. The fees payable by suitors under the tariff shall be paid over, by the officer appointed to collect them, to the Minister of Finance and Receiver General, and shall form part of the Consolidated Revenue Fund of Canada ; and the emoluments of the surrogate judge shall be paid therefrom. 40 V., c. 21, ss. 11, 12 and 14.

Judges to take oath of office.

8. Every judge and surrogate judge appointed in pursuance of this Act, shall, previously to his executing the duties of his office, take, before a judge of any superior or county court in Ontario, an oath in the form following, that is to say :

Form of oath.

"I do sincerely and solemnly "swear that I will duly and faithfully, and to the best of my "skill and knowledge, execute the powers and trusts reposed in "me as judge (*or* as a surrogate judge, *as the case may be*) of "the Maritime Court of Ontario. So help me God." 40 V., c. 21, s. 17.

OFFICERS.

Appointment of officers.

9. The Governor in Council may appoint a registrar, marshal, deputy registrars and deputy marshals, and examiners and other necessary officers for the court, with such of the powers belonging to registrars and marshals of British Vice-Admiralty Courts, and such other powers for the effectual working of this Act as are prescribed by general rules. 40 V., c. 21, s. 15.

And of assessors.

10. The judge shall, from time to time, submit, for the approval of the Minister of Justice, a list of persons of nautical or engineering, or other technical skill and experience, to act as assessors in the court ; and shall cause the approved list to be published in the *Canada Gazette*, and every person named in the approved list shall attend the court, under such circumstance and in such rotation, and subject to such regulations, and shall receive such fees, as are provided by general rules. 40 V., c. 21, s. 10.

BARRISTERS AND PROCTORS.

Who may practice in court.

11. All persons entitled to act as barristers or advocates in any superior court in any Province of Canada may act as such in the court ; and all persons entitled to practice as solicitors or

attorneys-at-law, in Ontario, may practice as proctors or solicitors in the court; and all persons acting as barristers, advocates, proctors, or solicitors in the court, shall be officers thereof. 40 V., c. 21, s. 18.

12. The principal seat of the court shall be at Toronto, but sittings of the court may be held at any city, town or place within the Province of Ontario. 40 V., c. 21, s. 4. **Where sittings may be held.**

JURISDICTION AND PROCEDURE.

13 Except as herein otherwise provided, all persons shall have, in the Province of Ontario, the like rights and remedies in all matters including cases of contract and tort and proceedings *in rem* and *in personam* arising out of or connected with navigation, shipping, trade or commerce on any river, lake, canal or inland water, of which the whole or part is in the Province of Ontario, as such persons would have in any existing British Vice-Admiralty Court if the process of such Court extended to the said Province. 40 V., c. 21, s. 1. **Rights and remedies in Ontario as to matters respecting shipping, &c.**

14. Subject to the provisions in this section contained, the court, for the enforcement of such rights and remedies, shall, as to the matters mentioned in the next preceding section, have all such jurisdiction as belongs to any existing British Vice-Admiralty Court in similar matters within the reach of its process: **Jurisdiction of the court.**

2. In any such matter arising within reach of the process of the Vice-Admiralty Court at Quebec, the court shall have the same jurisdiction as any existing British Vice-Admiralty Court has under like circumstances, in any like matter arising beyond the reach of its process: **As to matter arrising in Quebec.**

3. The jurisdiction of the court in respect of claims touching the ownership, possession, employment or earnings of ships, shall extend to the case of a ship registered in a port in the Province of Quebec, but navigating the waters aforesaid: **Jurisdiction as to ships registered at a port of Quebec.**

4. The court shall not have jurisdiction, save as aforesaid, in any matter to which the process of any existing British Vice-Admiralty Court extends,—nor shall the court have jurisdiction in any prize cause, or in any criminal matter, or in any case of breach of the regulations and instructions relating to Her Majesty's navy, or arising out of droits of Admiralty, or out of any seizure for breach of the revenue, customs, trade or navigation laws, or out of any violation of the Act of the Parliament of the United Kingdom, known as "*The Foreign Enlistment Act,*" or of the laws relating to the abolition of the slave trade, or to the capture and destruction of pirates and piratical vessels: **No jurisdiction in certain cases.**

5. No right or remedy *in rem* given by this Act only shall be enforced as against any subsequent *bona fide* purchaser or mortgagee of a ship, unless the proceedings for the enforcement thereof are begun within ninety days from the time when the same accrued: **Limitation as to remedies given by this Act only.**

6. No right or remedy *in rem* given by this Act, except a right or remedy *in rem* for the wages of seamen and other persons **Rights of certain**

mortgagees protected.

employed on board a ship on any river, lake, canal or inland water, of which the whole or part is in the Province of Ontario, shall be enforced as against any *bona fide* mortgagee under a mortgage duly executed and registered prior to the first day of October, one thousand eight hundred and seventy-eight. 40 V., c. 21, s. 2, part, s. 3;—42 V., c. 40, s. 1;—45 V., c. 34, s. 1.

Practice in cases unprovided for in rules.

15. The practice, pleading, writs and procedure in force at the time of its abolition in the instance side of the High Court of Admiralty in England shall, so far as applicable, apply and extend to proceedings instituted under this Act, when no other provision is made by this Act or the general rules made under this Act. 40 V., c. 21, s. 9.

Effect of decrees and orders of the judge.

16. All decrees and orders of the court, or of the judge or a surrogate judge thereof, whereby any moneys are payable to any person, shall have the same effect as decrees of the Court of Chancery in Ontario had on the sixteenth day of April, in the year one thousand eight hundred and seventy-eight,—and all powers of enforcing its decrees then possessed by the said Court of Chancery or any judge thereof, with respect to matters pending in that court, are hereby conferred on the court with respect to matters therein pending,—and all remedies possessed on that date by those to whom money was payable under a decree of the said Court of Chancery, are hereby conferred on persons to whom any moneys are payable by orders or decrees of the court, or of the judge or a surrogate judge thereof. 41 V., c. 1, s. 1.

Continuation of proceedings begun before surrogate Judge.

17. Any judicial act begun or partly proceeded with by a surrogate judge may, under general rules, be proceeded with or completed by the judge. 40 V., c. 21, s. 13.

Appeal to Supreme Court.

18. An appeal shall lie to the Supreme Court of Canada from every decision of the court having the force and effect of a definitive sentence or final order. 40 V., c. 21, s. 19.

Procedure in such appeal.

19. The practice, procedure and powers as to costs, and otherwise, of the Supreme Court of Canada in other appeals shall. so so far as applicable, and unless such court otherwise orders, apply and extend to appeals under this Act, when no other provision is made, either by this Act or the general rules made under this Act, or under "*The Supreme and Exchequer Courts Act.*" 40 V., c. 21, s. 20.

GENERAL PROVISIONS.

By whom oaths may be administered.

20. The judge, any surrogate judge, the registrar, any deputy-registrar, and any person who has power to administer oaths and affirmations in matters pending in the Supreme Court of Canada, or the Exchequer Court of Canada, may administer oaths and affirmations in relation to any matter pending in the court. 40 V., c. 21, s. 16, *part.*

Rules of practice and tariff of fees may be made.

21. The judge may, with the approval of the Governor in Council, from time to time, make, alter and rescind general rules for establishing and regulating the practice, pleading, writs, procedure, costs and fees to practitioners and officers in suits instituted under this Act, and for the effectual working of this Act; and such rules may extend to any matter of procedure, or otherwise, not provided for by this Act, but for which it is found necessary to provide, in order to insure the proper working of this Act and the better attainment of the objects thereof; and every such rule, not being inconsistent with the express provisions of this Act, shall have force and effect as if herein enacted: **Their effect.**

2. Copies of all such rules shall, as soon as possible, be laid before both Houses of Parliament, and entered on the records of the court, and published in the *Canada Gazette:* **Copies for Parliament.**

3. The Governor in Council may, by proclamation published in the *Canada Gazette*, or either House of Parliament may, by a resolution passed at any time within thirty days after such rules and orders have been laid before Parliament, suspend any rule or order made under this Act; and such rule or order shall thereupon cease to have force or effect until the end of the then next session of Parliament. 40 V., c. 21, s. 8. **Rule or order may be suspended.**

51 VICTORIA, CAP. 39.

An Act to extend the jurisdiction of the Maritime Court of Ontario.

[Assented to 22nd May, 1888.]

Preamble.

WHEREAS it is expedient to extend the powers and jurisdiction of the Maritime Court of Ontario: Therefore Her Majesty, by and with the advice and consent of the Senate and House of Commons of Canada, enacts as follows:

Jurisdiction as to mortgages.

1. The Maritime Court of Ontario shall have jurisdiction over, any claim in, respect of any mortgage upon any ship or vessel now or hereafter duly registered in the Province of Ontario, whether the ship or vessel, or the proceeds thereof, be under arrest of the court or not.

Exercise of jurisdiction.

2. The jurisdiction conferred by this Act may be exercised by proceedings *in rem* or *in personam*.

EXTRACT FROM "THE VICE ADMIRALTY COURTS ACT, 1863," showing matters in respect of which Vice Admiralty Courts have jurisdiction:

10. The Matters in respect of which the Vice Admiralty Courts shall have Jurisdiction are as follows: **Jurisdiction of Vice Admiralty Courts.**

(1.) Claims for Seamen's Wages:
(2.) Claims for Master's Wages, and for his Disbursements on account of the ship:
(3.) Claims in respect of Pilotage:
(4.) Claims in respect of Salvage of any ship, or of life or Goods therefrom:
(5.) Claims in respect of Towage:
(6.) Claims for Damage done by any Ship:
(7.) Claims in respect of Bottomry or Respondentia Bonds:
(8.) Claims in respect of any Mortgage where the Ship has been sold by a Decree of the Vice Admiralty Court and the Proceeds are under its Control:
(9.) Claims between the Owners of any Ship registered in the Possession, in which the Court is established, touching the Ownership, Possession, Employment, or Earnings of such Ship:
(10.) Claims for Necessaries supplied, in the Possession in which the Court is established, to any Ship of which no Owner or Part Owner is domiciled within the Possession at the Time of the Necessaries being supplied.
(11.) Claims in respect of the building, equipping, or repairing within any *British* Possession of any Ship of which no Owner or Part Owner is domiciled within the Possession at the Time of the Work being done.

11. The Vice Admiralty Courts shall also have Jurisdiction— **Jurisdiction of Vice Admiralty Courts.**

(1.) In all Cases of Breach of the Regulations and Instructions relating to Her Majesty's Navy at Sea:
(2.) In all Matters arising out of Droits of Admiralty.

12. Nothing contained in this Act shall be construed to take away or restrict the Jurisdiction conferred upon any Vice Admiralty Court by any Act of Parliament, in respect of Seizures for Breach of the Revenue, Customs, Trade, or Navigation Laws, or the Laws relating to the Abolition of the Slave Trade, or to the Capture and Destruction of Pirates and Piratical Vessels, or any other Jurisdiction now lawfully exercised by any such Court; or any Jurisdiction now lawfully exercised by any other Court within Her Majesty's Dominions. **Nothing to restrict existing Jurisdictions.**

13. The Jurisdiction of the Vice Admiralty Courts, except where it is expressly confined by this Act to matters arising within the Possession in which the Court is established, may be exercised, whether the Cause or Right of Action has arisen within or beyond the Limits of such Possession. **As to Matters arising beyond Limits of possession.**

SCHEDULE TO VICE ADMIRALTY ACT.

List of the existing Vice Admiralty Courts to which the Act applies.

Antigua.
Bahamas.
Barbadoes.
Bermuda.
British Columbia.
British Guiana.
British Honduras.
Cape of Good Hope.
Ceylon.
Dominica.
Falkland Islands.
Gambia River.
Gibraltar.
Gold Coast.
Grenada.
Hong Kong.
Jamaica.
Labuan.
Lagos.
Lower Canada, otherwise Quebec.
Malta.
Mauritius.
Montserrat
Natal.
Nevis.
New Brunswick.
Newfoundland.
New South Wales.
New Zealand.
Nova Scotia, otherwise Halifax.
Prince Edward Island.
Queensland.
Saint Christopher.
Saint Helena.
Saint Lucia.
Saint Vincent.
Sierra Leone.
South Australia.
Tasmania, formerly called Van Diemen's Land.
Tobago.
Trinidad.
Vancouver's Island.
Victoria.
Virgin Islands, otherwise Tortola.
Western Australia.

MARITIME COURT OF ONTARIO.

GENERAL RULES.

Government House, Ottawa,
The 14th day of February, 1889.

On the recommendation of the Minister of Justice and under the provisions of Chapter 137 of the Revised Statutes of Canada, intituled "The Maritime Court Act,"

His Excellency in Council has been pleased to order that the following rules and regulations made by the Judge of the said Court be and the same are hereby approved and adopted :—

GENERAL RULES.

I.—*Interpretation.*

Section 1. In these rules, together with the annexed schedules, the following words shall have the meanings hereby assigned to them, unless there be something in the subject matter or context repugnant to such construction, viz :— Interpretation.

(*a.*) Words importing the singular number shall include the plural, and words importing the plural number shall include the singular. Singular or plural number.

(*b.*) Words importing the masculine gender shall include females, and shall apply to bodies corporate as well as to individuals. Masculine gender.

(*c,*) "The Act" shall mean "The Maritime Court Act." The Act.

(*d.*) "Court" shall mean "The Maritime Court of Ontario." Court.

(*e.*) "Judge" shall mean the Judge of the said Court for the time being, or other person lawfully authorized to discharge the duties of the Judge. Judge.

(*f.*) "Surrogate" shall mean a surrogate Judge appointed by the Governor in Council under the Act, or other person lawfully authorized to discharge the duties of the surrogate Judge. Surrogate.

(*g.*) "Registrar" shall mean the registrar of the said Court for the time being, or other person lawfully authorized to discharge the duties of the registrar. Registrar.

(*h.*) "Deputy registrar" shall mean a deputy registrar appointed by the Governor in Council at the city, town, or place where a surrogate Judge shall have been appointed; or other person lawfully authorized to discharge the duties of the deputy registrar. Deputy registrar.

Marshal. (*j.*) "Marshal" shall mean the marshal of the Court for the time being, or other person lawfully authorized to discharge the duties of the marshal.

Deputy marshal. (*k.*) "Deputy marshal" shall mean a deputy marshal appointed by the Governor in Council, at the city, town or place where a surrogate Judge shall have been appointed; or other person lawfully authorized to discharge the duties of the deputy marshal.

Examiner. (*l.*) "Examiner" shall mean an examiner appointed under the Act by the Governor in Council.

Action. (*m.*) "Action" shall mean any action, cause, suit or other proceeding instituted in the Court.

Counsel. (*n.*) "Counsel" shall mean and include any barrister or advocate entitled to plead in the Court.

Solicitor. (*o.*) "Solicitor" shall mean and include any attorney, solicitor or proctor entitled to practice in the said Court, or the party himself if conducting his cause in person.

Party or person. (*p.*) "Party" or "person" shall include a corporation or other public body.

Oath. (*q.*) "Oath," "affidavit" and "swear" shall respectively include affirmation, declaration, affirm and declare, in the case of persons allowed by law to affirm and declare instead of swearing.

Ship. (*r.*) "Ship" shall include every description of vessel used in navigation not propelled by oars only.

Month. (*s.*) "Month shall mean a calendar month.

Registry. (*t.*) "Registry" shall mean the office of the registrar or of any deputy registrar.

II.—*Short Title.*

Short title. Sec. **2**. In referring to these rules it shall be a sufficient designation to use the expression "The Maritime Court Rules of Ontario."

III.—*Actions.*

Actions of two kinds. Sec. **3**. Actions shall be of two kinds, actions *in rem* and actions *in personam.*

Actions shall be numbered. Sec. **4**. All actions shall be numbered in the order in which they are instituted, and the number given to any action shall be the distinguishing number of the action, and shall be written or printed on all documents in the action as part of the title thereof. Forms of the title of an action will be found in schedule A hereto, Nos. 1 and 2.

IV.—*Writ of Summons.*

Writ to be indorsed with statement, &c. Sec. **5**. Every action shall be commenced by a writ of summons, which, before being issued, shall be indorsed with a statement of the nature of the claim, and of the relief or remedy required, and of the amount claimed, if any: such amount may include as part thereof the reasonable and probable amount of the costs to be incurred for the recovery of the claim. Forms of writ of summons and of the indorsements thereon will be found in schedule A hereto, Nos. 3, 4, 5, and 6.

When indorsement may include claim to have an account taken.

Sec. 6. In an action for seaman's or master's wages, or for master's wages and disbursements or for necessaries, or for bottomry, or in any mortgage action, or in any action in which the plaintiff desires an account, the indorsement on the writ of summons may include a claim to have an account taken.

Address for service to be indorsed.

Sec. 7. The writ of summons shall be indorsed with the name and address of the plaintiff, and of his solicitor, if any, and if he sues in person with an address, to be called *an address for service* not more than three miles from the registry, at which it shall be sufficient to leave all documents required to be served upon him.

Preparation and issue of writ.

Sec. 8. The writ of summons shall be prepared and indorsed by the plaintiff, and shall be issued under the seal of the Court, and a copy of the writ and of all the indorsements thereon, signed by the plaintiff, shall be left in the registry at the time of sealing the writ.

Amendment of writ and indorsements

Sec. 9. The Judge or surrogate may allow the plaintiff to amend the writ of summons and the indorsements thereon in such manner and on such terms as to the Judge or surrogate shall seem fit.

V.—*Service of Writ of Summons.*

Service in action *in rem.*

Sec. 10. In an action *in rem*, the writ of summons shall be served:—

Upon ship, or cargo &c., on board ship.

(*a.*) Upon ship, or upon cargo or other property, if the cargo or other property is on board a ship, by attaching the writ for a short time to the main-mast or the single mast, or to some other conspicuous part of the ship, and by leaving a copy of the writ attached thereto.

Upon cargo, &c., not on board ship.

(*b.*) Upon cargo or other property, if the cargo or other property is not on board a ship, by attaching the writ for a short time to such cargo or property, and by leaving a copy of the writ attached thereto.

Upon freight.

(*c.*) Upon freight in the hands of any person, by showing the writ to him and by leaving with him a copy thereof.

Upon proceeds in court

(*d.*) Upon proceeds in Court, by showing the writ to the registrar and by leaving with him a copy thereof.

If access cannot be obtained.

Sec. 11. If access cannot be obtained to the property on which it is to be served, the writ may be served by showing it to any person appearing to be in charge of such property, and by leaving with him a copy of the writ.

Service in action *in personam*.

Sec. 12. In an action *in personam*, the writ of summons shall be served by showing it to the defendant, and by leaving with him a copy of the writ.

Upon member or manager of a firm.

Sec. **13**. A writ of summons against a firm may be served upon any member of the firm, or upon any person appearing at the time of service to have the management of the business of the firm.

Against a corporation or public company.

Sec. **14**. A writ of summons against a corporation or a public company may be served in the mode, if any, provided by law for service of any other writ or legal process upon such corporation or company.

Service upon the president, manager, cashier, treasurer or secretary of corporation

Sec. **15**. Where no such provision exists, a writ of summons against a corporation may be served upon the president, manager, or other head officer, or upon the cashier, clerk, treasurer, or secretary of the corporation at the head office or at any branch or agency in Ontario, or on any other person discharging the like duties, and a writ of summons against a public company may be served upon the secretary of the company, or may be left at the office of the company.

If person to be served is under disability or prompt service can not be effected.

Sec. **16**. If the person to be served is under disibility, or if for any cause personal service cannot, or cannot promptly, be effected, or if in any action, whether *in rem* or *in personam*, there is any doubt or difficulty as to the person to be served, or as to the mode of service, the Judge or surrogate may order upon whom or in what manner service is to be made, or may order notice to be given in lieu of service.

Writ may be served by plaintiff or his agent within 6 months.

Sec. **17**. The writ of summons whether, *in rem* or *in personam*, may be served by the plaintiff or his agent within *six months* from the date thereof, and shall, after service, be filed with an affidavit of service indorsed thereon or attached thereto.

Affidavit of service.

Sec. **18**. The affidavit shall state the date and mode of service, and shall be sworn to by the person who served the writ. A form of affidavit of service will be found in schedule A hereto, No. 7.

Proceedings *in rem* in registry outside Toronto, certificate to be forwarded to registrar, containing certain particulars.

Sec. **19**. In all proceedings *in rem* in any registry outside Toronto it shall be the duty of the deputy registrar forthwith after the issuing of any writ of summons to forward to the registrar at Toronto a certificate of the fact of the issue of such writ, which certificate shall contain the number of the action, the names of the plaintiffs, the property proceeded against, the name of the owner, the amount of the claim, and whether a warrant has issued.

In case of decree and sale in an action instituted outside Toronto certificate to be forwarded to registrar containing particulars.

Sec. **20**. In every action instituted in a registry outside Toronto under which a decree has been made and under which a sale of the vessel is effected, the deputy registrar shall forward to the registrar at Toronto a eertificate of such fact: And the said certificate shall mention the number of the suit, the names of the plaintiffs and the owners, and the name of the vessel, together with the amount realized on the sale, and the name of the purchaser.

Upon receipt of the certificate registrar shall make entry of contents thereof.

Sec. **21**. Upon the receipt of the certificate mentioned in the two next preceeding sections the registrar shall enter in a book which he shall keep for the purpose the contents of the said certificate, duly indexing the same under the names of the plaintiff, owner, and the vessel. And the registrar shall enter in the same book similar particulars as to all actions commenced in his own office.

VI.—*Appearance.*

Sec. **22.** A party appearing to a writ of summons shall file an appearance at the place directed in the writ. Appearance to be filed.

Sec. **23.** A party not appearing within the time limited by the writ may, by consent of the other parties or by permission of the judge or surrogate appear at any time on such terms as the judge or surrogate shall order. Appearance on terms on expiry of time.

Sec. **24.** If the party appearing has a set-off or counterclaim against the plaintiff, he may indorse on his appearance a statement of the nature thereof, and of the relief or remedy required, and of the amount, if any, of the set-off or counterclaim. But if in the opinion of the judge or surrogate such set-off or counterclaim cannot be conveniently disposed of in the action, the judge or surrogate may order it to be struck out. Indorsement of set-off or counterclaim on appearance.

Sec. **25.** The appearance shall be signed by the party appearing, and shall state his name and address, and those of his solicitor, if any, and if he appears in person also an address, to be called *an address for service* not more than three miles from the registry, at which it shall be sufficient to leave all documents required to be served upon him. Forms of appearance and of indorsement of set-off or counterclaim will be found in Schedule A hereto, Nos. 8 and 9. Address for service to be indorsed on appearance.

VII.—*Parties.*

Sec. **26.** Any number of persons having interests of the same nature arising out of the same matter may be joined in the same action whether as plaintiffs or as defendants. Number of persons may be joined.

Sec. **27.** The judge or surrogate may order any person who is interested in the action, though not named in the writ of summons, to come in either as plaintiff or as defendant. Adding a person interested.

Sec. **28.** For the purposes of the last preceding section an underwriter or insurer or mortgagee shall be deemed to be a person interested in the action. Who deemed a person interested.

Sec. **29.** The judge or surrogate may order upon what terms any person shall come in, and what notices and documents, if any, shall be given to and served upon him, and may give such further directions in the matter as to him shall seem fit. Terms upon which person may be made a party.

VIII.—*Consolidation of Actions.*

Sec. **30.** Two or more actions in which the questions at issue are substantially the same, or for matters which might properly be combined in one action, may be consolidated by order of the judge or surrogate upon such terms as to him shall seem fit. Action may be consolidated upon terms to be fixed by judge or surrogate.

Several actions may be tried at same time. Same evidence. Test action.

Sec. **31**. The judge or surrogate if he thinks fit, may order several actions to be tried at the same time, and on the same evidence, or the evidence in one action to be used as evidence in another, or may order one of several actions to be tried as a test action, and the other actions to be stayed to abide the result.

Two or more actions brought against the same property, how consolidated and how dissevered.

Sec. **32**. If two or more actions be brought against the same property the writs for which have been issued from the same office, the judge or surrogate as the case may be, may consolidate the same, and may afterwards if necessary dissever the actions; but an application for the consolidation of, or afterwards for the disseverance of two or more actions, wherein all the writs have not been issued from the same office, shall be made to the judge.

Action and cross action may be heard at the same time.

Sec. **33**. Action and cross action of damage may be directed by the judge or surrogate, as the case may be, to be heard at the same time, and upon the same evidence, but if the actions be not commenced in the same office the order for the trial shall be made by the judge.

IX.— *Warrants.*

Warrant in an action *in rem*, how issued and what facts to state.

Sec. **34**. In an action *in rem*, a warrant for the arrest of property may be issued by the registrar or deputy registrar at the time of, or at any time after the issue of the writ of summons, on an affidavit being filed, stating the facts as prescribed by the following sections. Forms of affidavit to lead warrant will be found in schedule A hereto, Nos. 10, 11 and 12.

Affidavit, what to state.

Sec. **35**. The affidavit shall state the nature of the claim, and that the aid of the court is required.

Sec. **36**. The affidavit shall also state :—

In action for wages, &c.

(*a.*) In an action for wages, the national character of the ship, and if the ship is foreign, that notice of the action has been served upon a consular officer of the State to which the ship belongs, if there is one resident at Toronto or in the place where the writ is issued;

In action for necessaries, or for building, &c.

(*b.*) In an action for necessaries, or for building, equipping, or repairing any ship, the national character of the ship, and that, to the best of the deponent's belief, no owner or part owner of the ship was domiciled in the Province of Ontario at the time when the necessaries were supplied or the work was done;

In action between co-owners.

(*c.*) In an action between co-owners relating to the ownership, possession, employment, or earnings of any ship registered in the Province of Ontario or the Province of Quebec, the port at which the ship is registered and the number of shares in the ship owned by the party proceeding.

In a mortgage action.

(*d.*) In a mortgage action, the nationality of the mortgagee and verifying a copy of the mortgage annexed to the affidavit.

In an action for bottomry

Sec. **37**. In an action for bottomry, the bottomry bond in original, and, if it is in a foreign language, a translation thereof, shall be produced for the inspection and perusal of the registrar or deputy registrar, and a copy of the bond, or of the translation thereof, certified to be correct, shall be annexed to the affidavit.

Sec. **38**. The registrar, or deputy registrar, if he thinks fit, may issue a warrant, although the affidavit does not contain all the prescribed particulars, and, in an action for bottomry, although the bond has not been produced; or he may refuse to issue a warrant without the order of the Judge or surrogate. **Issue of warrant though affidavit does not contain all the prescribed particulars.**

Sec. **39**. The warrant shall be prepared in the registry, and shall be signed by the registrar, or deputy registrar, and issued under the seal of the Court. A form of warrant will be found in schedule A hereto, No. 13. **Warrant, where prepared and by whom signed.**

Sec. **40**. The warrant shall be addressed to the marshal and to each deputy marshal of the Court and shall be delivered to such of them as the registrar or deputy registrar may, with a view of saving expense, think best, and shall be executed by him or his substitutes. Immediately after execution the warrant shall be returned by the marshal or deputy marshal and filed with the registrar or deputy registrar who issued the same, with a certificate of service indorsed thereon, and notice of the execution thereof shall be given by the marshal or deputy marshal to the solicitor who issued same. **Warrant, to whom addressed and delivered.** **Execution and return and filing of warrant with certificate of service and notice.**

Sec. **41**. The warrant shall be served by the marshal, deputy marshal or other officer in the manner prescribed by these rules for the service of a writ of summons in an action *in rem* and thereupon the property shall be deemed to be arrested. **Warrant to be served by marshal or deputy marshal.**

Sec. **42**. The warrant may be served on Sunday, Good Friday, Christmas Day or any public holiday as well as on any other day. **Service on Sunday or holiday.**

Sec. **43**. The certificate shall state by whom the warrant has been served, and the date and mode of service, and shall be signed by the marshal or deputy marshal. A form of certificate of service will be found in schedule A hereto, No. 14. **Certificate of service, what to state.**

Sec. **44**. Whenever the property to be arrested is at a distance from the marshal or any deputy marshal, the registrar or deputy registrar may, with a view of saving expense, address the warrant to some literate person in the neighborhood of the property, in which case such person shall, with respect to the warrant, perform the same duties and be entitled to the same fees as the marshal or deputy marshal would have performed and been entitled to had the warrant been executed by him. **Service when property to be arrested is distant from marshal or deputy marshal may be made by some literate person.**

Sec. **45**. The registrar or deputy registrar shall wherever a warrant is addressed to a person other than the marshal or deputy marshal give to such person all necessary instructions as to the execution thereof. **Necessary instructions in such case.**

X.—*Two or more actions against the Same Property.*

Sec. **46**. When the property is under arrest of the Court, if there be a second or subsequent action against the same property, **Second or subsequent action against** property under arrest.

it shall not be necessary to take out a warrant for the further arrest thereof, but if in such second or subsequent action such requirements as wonld have entitled the plaintiff to a warrant had the property not been under arrest be complied with, the property shall be held as under arrest in such second or subsequent action also, and the registrar, or deputy registrar as the case may be, shall issue his certificate to that effect, and an office copy of such certificate shall be annexed to and served with the copy of the writ to be served. (1)

Action against property under arrest commenced in another office; provisions and requirements in such case.

Sec. **47**. If when any property is under arrest of the Court, there be another action against the same property which has been commenced in another office, it shall not be necessary to take out a warrant for the further arrest thereof; but if in such other action such requirements as would have entitled the plaintiff to a warrant had the property not been under arrest be complied with, the registrar or deputy registrar, as the case may be, shall issue his certificate to that effect, which certificate shall be filed with the registrar or deputy registrar who issued the warrant under which the property has been arrested, and thereupon the property shall be held as under arrest in such other action and shall only be released upon the certificate of the registrar or deputy registrar with whom the other action has been instituted to the effect that the party seeking the release is entitled thereto. An office copy of the first-mentioned certificate shall be annexed to and served with the copy of the writ to be served in such other cause.

If bail is to be given in other action.

If bail is to be given in such other action the proceedings relating thereto are to be taken in the office of the registrar or deputy registrar with whom the action is instituted.

XI.—*Bail.*

Bail, how to be given.

Sec. **48**. Whenever bail is required by these rules, it shall be given by filing one or more bail bonds, each of which shall be signed by two sureties, unless the judge or surrogate shall, on special cause shown, order that one surety shall suffice. If bail is to be given the bond may be in the form number 15 of schedule A hereto.

Execution of bail bond and affidavits of execution and justification.

Sec. **49**. Such bond may be executed in the presence of one witness who must make an affidavit verifying the execution, the sureties must justify by affidavit, and the bail bond may be signed and the affidavits taken before any Commissioner of the Supreme Court of Judicature for the Province of Ontario. Form of affidavit of justification will be found in schedule A hereto No. 16.

Bond and affidavits to be filed.

Sec. **50**. Upon the bond being so executed it may, with the affidavits of execution and justification, be filed with the registrar or deputy registrar, as the case may be, and an appointment may be obtained for its consideration before him.

Notice of appointment for hearing parties relative o the suffi-

Twenty-four hours' notice of such appointment, together with the names and addresses of the sureties and the amount of the bond, shall be given to the plaintiff, unless the judge or surrogate for special reasons allow a shorter notice to be given, and on the

1 Citation in Rem. William Bruce p 196.

ciency of the sureties, how to be given and what to contain.

return of the appointment the registrar or deputy registrar may hear the parties and any evidence they may adduce regarding the sufficiency of the sureties, and may allow or disallow the bond. He may adjourn the appointment from time to time if he thinks necessary, and shall himself make such inquiries respecting the sureties as he thinks fit.

XII.—*Releases.*

Release for property arrested.

Sec. **51**. A release for property arrested by warrant may be issued by order of the judge or surrogate.

When it may be issued from registry.

Sec. **52**. A release may also be issued by the registrar or deputy registrar, unless there is a *caveat* outstanding against the release of the property :—

Payment into court.

(*a.*) On payment into court of the amount claimed, or of the appraised value of the property arrested, or where cargo is arrested for freight only, of the amount of the freight verified by affidavit ;

Bail bond being filed,

(*b.*) On one or more bail bonds being filed for the amount claimed, or for the appraised value of the property arrested ; and on proof that *twenty-four hours'* notice of the names and addresses of the sureties has been previously served on the party at whose instance the property has been arrested ;

Application of party.

(*c.*) On the application of the party at whose instance the property has been arrested ;

Consent in writing.

(*d.*) On a consent in writing being filed signed by the party at whose instance the property has been arrested ;

Discontinuance, &c.

(*e*) On discontinuance or dismissal of the action in which the property has been arrested.

Property arrested for salvage.

Sec. **53**. Where property has been arrested for salvage, the release shall not be issued under the next foregoing section, except on discontinuance or dismissal of the action, until the value of the property arrested has been agreed upon between the parties or determined by the judge or surrogate.

Registrar, &c. may refuse.

Sec. **54**. The registrar or deputy registrar may refuse to issue a release without the order of the judge or surrogate.

Preparation, signing and issue of release.

Sec. **55**. The release shall be prepared in the registry, and shall be signed by the registrar or deputy registrar, and issued under the seal of the court. A form of release will be found in schedule A hereto, No. 17.

Release, how served.

Sec. **56**. The release shall be served on the marshal or deputy marshal, either personally or by leaving it at his office, by the party by whom it is taken out.

Property free from arrest on service of release, &c.

Sec. **57**. On service of the release, and on payment to the marshal or deputy marshal of all fees due to and charges incurred by him in respect of the arrest and custody of the property, the property shall be at once released from arrest.

XIII.—*Preliminary Acts.*

Sec. **58**. In an action for damage by collision, each party shall, within *one week* from an appearance being entered, file a *preliminary act*, sealed up, signed by the party, and containing a statement of the following particulars :—

Names. (*a.*) The names of the ships which came into collision, and the names of their masters;

Time. (*b.*) The time of the collision;

Place. (*c.*) The place of the collision;

Wind. (*d.*) The direction and force of the wind;

Weather. (*e.*) The state of the weather;

Tide. (*f.*) The state and force of the tide (if the collision occurred in tidal waters);

Course and speed. (*g.*) The course and speed of the ship when the other was first seen;

Lights. (*h.*) The lights, if any, carried by her;

Distance and bearing. (*i.*) The distance and bearing of the other ship when first seen;

Lights first seen. (*j.*) The lights, if any, of the other ship which were first seen;

Other lights. (*k.*) The lights, if any, of the other ship, other than those first seen, which came into view before the collision;

Measures taken. (*l.*) The measures which were taken, and when, to avoid the collision;

Parts first collided with (*m.*) The parts of each ship which first came into collision;

Fault or default. (*n.*) What fault or default, if any, is attributed to the other ship.

XIV.—*Pleadings.*

No pleadings, when. Sec. **59**. Every action shall be heard without pleadings, unless the Judge or surrogate shall otherwise order.

Statement of claim, defence and reply to be filed within one week in each case. Sec. **60**. If an order is made for pleadings, the plaintiff shall within *one week* from the date of the order, file his statement of claim; and, within *one week* from the filing of the statement of claim, the defendant shall file his statement of defence; and, within *one week* from the filing of the statement of defence, the plaintiff shall file his reply, if any; and there shall be no pleading beyond the reply, except by permission of the Judge or surrogate.

What may be pleaded. Set-off or counterclaim. Sec. **61**. The defendant may, in his statement of defence, plead any set-off or counterclaim. But if, in the opinion of the Judge or surrogate, such set-off or counterclaim can not be conveniently disposed of in the action, the Judge or surrogate may order it to be struck out.

Sec. **62**. Every pleading shall be divided into short paragraphs numbered consecutively, which shall state concisely the facts on which the party relies; and all the pleadings in a cause must be filed at the same office.

Paragraphs to be numbered; and all pleadings filed in same office.

Sec. **63**. It shall not be necessary to set out in any pleading the words of any document referred to therein, except so far as the precise words of the document are material.

Words of document, how set out.

Sec. **64**. The form of pleadings and the legal effect of the same and the practice in relation thereto shall, subject to the provisions of these rules, be the same as that directed by the rules of practice in force from time to time in the Supreme Court of Judicature for Ontario; or the forms of pleadings appended to the rules of the Vice-Admiralty Courts established by the Queen's Order in Council of the 23rd August, 1883, may be used.

Rules of Supreme Court for Ontario and of British Vice-Admiralty Courts, how far applicable.

Sec. **65**. Either party may apply to the Judge or surrogate to decide forthwith any question of fact or of law raised by any pleading, and the Judge or surrogate shall thereupon make such order as to him shall seem fit.

Question of law or fact may be decided forthwith.

Sec. **66**. Any pleading may at any time be amended, either by consent of the parties, or by order of the Judge or surrogate.

Amendment of pleading.

Sec. **67**. All writs, pleadings, notices, orders, warrants and other documents and written communications which do not require personal service upon the party to be affected thereby, may be served upon his solicitor or upon the agent of such solicitor named in the "solicitor's and agent's book" provided for by section 265 of these rules, and kept in the office of the registrar or deputy registrar from which the writ issued. And if any such solicitor neglects to cause the name of his agent to be specified in such book, the posting up a copy of any such writ, pleading, notice, order, warrant or other document or written communication for the solicitor so neglecting as aforesaid, in the office of the registrar or deputy registrar, as the case may be, is to be deemed sufficient service.

Service of writs, pleadings, notices, &c., not requiring personal service, how made.

Posting up copy in office of registry, when sufficient service.

XV.—*Interrogatories.*

Sec. **68**. At any time before the action is set down for hearing any party desirous of obtaining the answers of the adverse party on any matters material to the issue, may apply to the judge or surrogate for leave to administer interrogatories to the adverse party to be answered on oath, and the judge or surrogate may direct within what time and in what way they shall be answered, whether by affidavit or by oral examination.

Leave to administer interrogatories. When and how to be obtained.

Sec. **69**. The judge or surrogate may order any interrogatory that he considers objectionable to be amended or struck out; and if the party interrogated omits to answer or answers insufficiently, the judge or surrogate may order him to answer, or to answer further, and either by affidavit or by oral examination. Forms of interrogatories and of answers will be found in schedule A hereto, Nos. 18 and 19.

Objectionable interrogatory may be amended or struck out.

XVI.—*Discovery and Inspection.*

Discovery on oath, how obtained.

Sec. **70.** The judge or surrogate may order any party to an action to make discovery, on oath, of all documents which are in his possession or power relating to any matter in question therein.

Affidavit of discovery.

Sec. **71.** The affidavit of discovery shall specify which, if any, of the documents therein mentioned the party objects to produce.

Notice for inspection or transcription.

Sec. **72.** Any party to an action may file a notice to any other party to produce, for inspection or transcription, any document in his possession or power relating to any matter in question in the action.

Order to produce, how obtained.

Sec. **73.** If the party served with notice to produce omits or refuses to do so within the time specified in the notice, the adverse party may apply to the judge or surrogate for an order to produce.

XVII.—*Examination of Parties.*

Rules, &c. of Supreme Court of Ontario to apply.

Sec. **74.** Any party to an action may be examined by the party adverse in interest, and the practice thereon shall be the same as that directed by the rules and practice of the Supreme Court of Judicature of Ontario in that behalf.

XVIII.—*Admission of Documents and Facts.*

Notice to admit document or fact may be filed.

Sec. **75.** Any party may file a notice to any other party to admit any document or fact (saving all just exceptions), and a party not admitting it after such notice shall be liable for the costs of proving the document or fact, whatever the result of the action may be, unless the taxing officer is of opinion that there was sufficient reason for not admitting it.

No costs unless notice be given.

Sec. **76.** No costs of proving any document shall be allowed, unless notice to admit shall have been previously given, or the taxing officer shall be of opinion that the omission to give such notice was reasonable and proper.

XIX—*Special Case.*

Special case by agreement.

Sec. **77.** Parties may agree to state the questions at issue for the opinion of the judge or surrogate in the form of a special case.

Question of law may be raised by order of judge or surrogate.

Sec. **78.** If it appears to the judge or surrogate that there is in any action a question of law which it would be convenient to have decided in the first instance, he may direct that it shall be raised in a special case or in such other manner as he may deem expedient.

Special case, how divided and stated.

Sec. **79.** Every special case shall be divided into paragraphs, numbered consecutively, and shall state concisely such facts and documents as may be necessary to enable the judge or surrogate to decide the question at issue.

Sec. **80**. Every special case shall be signed by the parties, and may be filed by any party. Signed by parties.

XX.—*Motions.*

Sec. **81**. A party desiring to obtain an order from the judge or surrogate shall file a notice of motion with the affidavits, if any, on which he intends to rely. Notice of motion.

Sec. **82**. The notice of motion shall state the nature of the order desired, the day on which the motion is to be made, and whether in court or in chambers. What notice of motion shall state.

Sec. **83**. Except by consent of the adverse party, or by order of the judge or surrogate, the notice of motion shall be filed *twenty-four hours* at least before the time at which the motion is made. When notice shall be filed.

Sec. **84**. All the affidavits upon which a notice of motion is founded must be filed before the service of the notice of motion; and affidavits in answer must be filed not later than the day before that appointed for the hearing of the motion. When affidavits for notice must be filed.

Sec. **85**. No motion shall be made to the judge or surrogate in court save by counsel or by a party conducting his own cause in person. Solicitors may be heard on any motion before the judge or surrogate in chambers. Motion in court. Solicitors in chambers.

Sec. **86**. Any notice of motion may be transferred from the chamber to the court list, or *vice versa*, as the judge or a surrogate may direct. Notice of motion may be transferred.

Sec. **87**. When the motion comes on for hearing, the judge or surrogate, after hearing the parties, or, in the absence of any of them, on proof that the notice of motion has been duly served, may make such order as to him shall seem fit. Order may be made of proof of service of notice.

Sec. **88**. The judge or surrogate may, on due cause shown, vary, or rescind any order previously made. Power to vary or rescind.

Sec. **89**. No proceeding shall be defeated by any formal objection. Formal objection.

Sec. **90**. All orders made by the judge or surrogate in chambers shall have the force and effect of orders of the court. Effect of order in chambers.

Sec. **91**. When the writ has been issued by the registrar all applications in the cause to the court or in chambers shall be heard by the judge, unless he direct the same to be heard before a surrogate. Hearing of applications when writ issued by registrar.

When the writ has been issued by a deputy registrar all applications in the cause to the court or in chambers shall be heard by the surrogate residing nearest the place where such deputy registrar's office is, unless he direct the same to be heard before the judge or another surrogate. Hearing of applications when writ issued by a deputy registrar.

XXI.—*Tenders.*

Payment into court and filing of notice in case of tender.

Sec. **92**. A party desiring to make a tender in satisfaction of the whole or any part of the adverse party's claim, shall pay into court the amount tendered by him, and shall file a notice of the terms on which the tender is made. A party may make a tender notwithstanding he has pleaded other grounds of defence.

Filing of notice by adverse party, accepting or rejecting.

Sec. **93**. Within *a week* from the filing of the notice of tender the adverse party shall file a notice, stating whether he accepts or rejects the tender, and if he shall not do so, he shall be held to have rejected it. Forms of notice of tender and of notice accepting or rejecting it will be found in schedule A hereto, Nos. 20 and 21.

Suspense of proceedings.

Sec. **94**. Pending the acceptance or rejection of a tender, the proceedings shall be suspended.

XXII.—*Evidence.*

Statutes of Ontario to apply.

Sec. **95**. The statutes respecting witnesses and evidence in force in the Province of Ontario shall apply to trials and proceedings in the Maritime Court.

Modes of giving evidence.

Sec. **96**. Evidence shall be given either by affidavit or by oral examination, or partly in one mode, and partly in another.

Evidence on motion and on hearing, subject to order of judge or a surrogate.

Sec. **97**. Evidence on a motion shall in general be given by affidavit, and at the hearing by the oral examination of witnesses; but the mode or modes in which evidence shall be given, either on any motion or at the hearing, may be determined either by consent of the parties, or by order of the judge or surrogate.

Order to attend for cross-examination.

Sec. **98**. The judge or surrogate may order any person who has made an affidavit in an action to attend for cross-examination thereon before the judge or surrogate, or the registrar or deputy registrar, or before an examiner named in the order.

The order and manner in which witnesses may be examined, &c.

Sec. **99**. Witnesses examined orally before the judge, surrogate, registrar or deputy registrar or examiner, shall be examined, cross-examined, and re-examined in such order as the judge, surrogate, registrar or deputy registrar or examiner, may direct; and questions may be put to any witness by the judge, surrogate, registrar or deputy registrar or examiner, as the case may be.

Examination by interpretation.

Sec. **100**. If any witness is examined by interpretation, such interpretation shall be made by a sworn interpreter of the court, or by a person previously sworn according to the form in schedule A hereto, No. 22.

Copies of examinations, how obtained.

Sec. **101**. The parties to the action shall, on payment of the regular fees, be entitled to have from the examiner certified copies of such depositions or any part thereof immediately after they have been taken.

Examination *viva voce* may be ordered.

Sec. **102**. Either solicitor in the action may apply to the judge or surrogate to order the attendance of any witness for examination *viva voce* at the hearing, although the witness may have already made an affidavit or been examined before the judge or surrogate, r an examiner or officer of the court.

XXIII.—*Oaths.*

Sec. **103**. The judge or surrogate may appoint any person to administer oaths in any particular proceeding in the Maritime Court. A form of appointment to administer oaths will be found in schedule A hereto, No. 23. Judge or surrogate may appoint.

XXIV.—*Affidavits.*

Sec. **104**. Every affidavit shall be divided into short paragraphs numbered consecutively, and shall be in the first person; and the name, address and description of every person making an affidavit shall be inserted therein. To be divided into paragraphs numbered.

Sec. **105**. The names of all the persons making an affidavit, and the dates when, and the places where it is sworn, shall be inserted in the jurat. Names, dates and places in jurat.

Sec. **106**. When an affidavit is made by any person who is blind, or who from his signature or other wise appears to be illiterate, the person before whom the affidavit is sworn shall certify that the affidavit was read over to the deponent, and that the deponent appeared to understand the same, and made his mark or wrote his signature thereto in the presence of the person before whom the affidavit was sworn. Affidavit by person blind or illiterate to be read over and certified.

Sec. **107**. When an affidavit is made by a person who does not speak the English language, the affidavit shall be taken down and read over to the deponent by interpretation either of a sworn interpreter of the court, or of a person previously sworn faithfully to interpret the affidavit. A form of jurat will be found in schedule A hercto, No. 24. Affidavit by interpretation, how made.

Sec. **108**. Affidavits may by permission of the judge or surrogate be used as evidence in an action, saving all just exceptions: Affidavits, before whom to be sworn.

(*a*.) If sworn to, in the United Kingdom of Great Britain and Ireland, or in any British possession, before any person authorized to administer oaths in the said United Kingdom or in such possession respectively; In British territory.

(*b*.) If sworn to, in any place not being a part of Her Majesty's dominions, before a British minister, consul, vice-consul, or notary public, or before a judge or magistrate the signature of such judge or magistrate being authenticated by the official seal of the court to which he is attached. In foreign territory.

Sec. **109**. The reception of any affidavit as evidence may be objected to, if the affidavit has been sworn before the solicitor for the party on whose behalf it is offered, or before a partner or clerk of such solicitor. When affidavit may be objected to.

XXV.—*Certificate of State of Action.*

Certificate of proceedings in office of registry.

Sec. **110**. Upon the application of any person the registrar or deputy registrar is to certify, as shortly as he conveniently can, the several proceedings had in his office in any action or matter, and the dates thereof.

XXVI.—*Examination of Witnesses before Trial.*

Judge or surrogate may order examination of witnesses before trial under certain circumstances.

Sec. **111**. The judge or surrogate may order that any witness, who cannot conveniently attend at the trial of the action or, if in the opinion of the judge or surrogate it may be impossible or very difficult to procure his attendance at the trial, shall be examined previously thereto, before either the judge or surrogate, or the registrar or deputy registrar, who shall have power to adjourn the examination from time to time, and from place to place, if he shall think necessary. A form of order for examination of witnesses will be found in schedule A hereto, No. 25.

Examination before special examiner or a commissioner.

Sec **112**. If the witness cannot be conveniently examined before the judge, surrogate or the registrar or deputy registrar, the judge or surrogate may order that he shall be examined before a special examiner, and if the witness is beyond the limits of the Province of Ontario, the judge or surrogate may order that he shall be examined before a commissioner specially appointed for the purpose.

Power to swear witnesses.

Sec. **113**. The examiner or commissioner shall have power to swear any witnesses produced before him for examination, and to adjourn, if necessary, the examination from time to time, and from place to place. A form of commission to examine witnesses will be found in schedule A hereto, No. 26.

Counsel fee on examination.

Sec. **114**. The parties, their counsel and solicitors, may attend the examination, but, if counsel attend, the fees of only one counsel on each side shall be allowed on taxation, except by order of the judge or surrogate.

Evidence to be taken in writing and certified.

Sec. **115**. The evidence of every witness shall be taken down in writing, and shall be certified as correct by the judge, surrogate, registrar or deputy registrar, or by the examiner or commissioner, as the case may be.

Evidence to be lodged in registry. Transmitted to registry

Sec. **116**. The certified evidence shall be lodged in the registry, or, if taken by commission, shall forthwith be transmitted by the commissioner to the registry, together with his commission. A form of return to commission to examine witnesses will be found in schedule A hereto, No. 27.

Evidence may be filed by either party.

Sec. **117**. As soon as the certified evidence has been received in the registry, it may be taken up and filed by either party, and may be used as evidence in the action, saving all just exceptions.

XXVII.—*Short-Hand.*

Examination taken in short-hand.

Sec. **118**. In case of an examination before the trial or otherwise than at the trial of an action, if the examining party desires to have such examination taken in short-hand, he shall be entitled to have it so taken at the place of examination except when the judge or surrogate sees fit to order otherwise.

Sec. **119**. When an examination in an action or proceeding in court or otherwise is taken by an examiner or other duly authorized person in short-hand the examination may be taken down by question and answer; and in such case it shall not be necessary for the depositions to be read over to or be signed by the person examined unless the judge or surrogate so directs where the examination is taken before the judge or surrogate, or in other cases unless any of the parties so desires. **Examination by question and answer, how to be taken.**

Sec. **120**. A copy of the depositions so taken, certified by the person taking the same as correct shall for all purposes have the same effect as the original depositions in ordinary cases. **Copy of depositions so taken.**

Sec. **121**. Except in cases where the examiner himself takes the examination in short-hand, the short-hand writer employed shall be previously sworn faithfully to report the evidence. A form of oath to be administered to the short-hand writer will be found in schedule A hereto, No. 28. **Short-hand writer to be sworn.**

Sec. **122**. The judge may from time to time appoint under the seal of the court an official reporter of the court, and it shall be his duty to attend all sittings of the court at Toronto, (or elsewhere if required by the judge), and report in short-hand the evidence and proceedings at trials at such sittings. **Appointment of official reporter.**

Sec. **123**. The official reporter shall be entitled for his attendance at court and for copies of evidence when ordered by either party or by the judge or surrogate to the fees set out in the table of fees in schedule B hereto. **Fees to official reporter.**

Sec. **124**. Every official reporter shall before entering on the duties of his office, take the following oath before the judge, and the same shall be filed in the registrar's office:— **Oath of office of official reporter.**

I, A. B., do solemnly and sincerely promise and swear that I will faithfully report the depositions and evidence and proceedings in any case in which it may be my duty to act as official reporter. So help me God.

Sec. **125**. The judge or surrogate may direct the evidence at any trial of an action to be taken in short-hand, and may make such order as to the costs of taking the same as to him shall seem just. **Short-hand evidence at trial may be ordered.**

XXVIII.--*Printing.*

Sec. **126**. The judge or surrogate may order that the whole of the pleadings and written proofs, or any part thereof, shall be printed before the trial; and the printing shall be in such form as the judge or surrogate shall order. **Printing of pleadings and written proofs.**

Sec. **127**. Preliminary acts, if printed, shall be printed in parallel columns. **Preliminary acts.**

XXIX.—*Assessors.*

Appointment of assessors.

Sec. **128**. The judge or surrogate, on the application of any party, or without any such application, if he considers that the nature of the case requires it, may appoint one or more assessors to advise the court upon any matters requiring nautical or other professional knowledge.

Assessor duly summoned three clear days shall give his attendance and assistance.
Summons shall be sent in registered letter.
Assessor failing to attend subject to removal.
In case of absence or illness of assessor.

Sec. **129**. Each assessor named in the list of assessors prepared under the Act on being duly summoned three clear days before the day on which his attendance is required, shall give his attendance and assistance accordingly; such summons shall be sent by the registrar or deputy registrar in a registered letter directed to the assessor at his address as specified in the list, or such other address as shall on the application of the assessor be substituted therefor in a copy of the list to be kept in the registrar's or deputy registrar's office. If any assessor being duly summoned shall, without reasonable excuse fail to attend or to give his assistance, the Minister of Justice, on the application of the judge, may remove his name from the list. The judge or surrogate shall have power, in case of the absence or illness of any assessor summoned, or for other cause which shall appear to him sufficient, to pass over such assessor and cause another to be summoned in his stead.

Assessors to be paid $6 per day, and the fees to be costs in the cause.

Sec. **130**. Each assessor shall be paid in each case the sum of six dollars for each day on which he shall attend in pursuance of any such summons for that purpose as aforesaid, and the fees of each assessor shall be costs in the cause; but shall in the first instance be paid by such of the parties to the action as the judge or surrogate may direct.

Assessors to be selected in rotation.

Sec. **131**. The assessors shall be selected from such list in rotation unless the judge or surrogate for any special reason shall otherwise direct.

XXX.—*Setting down for Trial.*

Filing notice of trial.

Sec. **132**. An action shall be set down for trial by filing a notice of trial. A form of notice of trial will be found in schedule A hereto, No. 29.

If there has been no appearance.

Sec. **133**. If there has not been any appearance, the plaintiff may set down the action for trial, on obtaining from the judge or surrogate leave to proceed *ex parte*:—

In an action *in personam*.

(*a*.) In an action *in personam*, or an action against proceeds in court, after the expiration of *two weeks* from the service of the writ of summons;

In an action *in rem*.

(*b*.) In an action *in rem* (not being an action against proceeds in court), after the expiration of *two weeks* from the filing of the warrant.

If an appearance.

Sec. **134**. If there has been appearance, either party may set down the action for trial;—

(*a.*) After the expiration of *one week* from the entry of the appearance, unless an order has been made for pleadings, or an application for such an order is pending; After expiration of one week.

(*b.*) If pleadings have been ordered, when the last pleading has been filed, or when the time allowed to the adverse party for filing any pleading has expired without such pleading having been filed. If pleadings have been ordered.

In collision cases the preliminary acts may be opened as soon as the action has been set down for trial. In collision cases.

Sec. **135**. Where the writ of summons has been endorsed with a claim to have an account taken, or the liability has been admitted or determined, and the question is simply as to the amount due, the judge or surrogate may, on the application of either party, fix a time within which the accounts and vouchers, and the proofs in support thereof, shall be filed, and at the expiration of that time either party may have the matter sent down for trial. Where claim to have account taken. When liability admitted, &c. Fixing a time for filing accounts, &c.

XXXI.—*Trial.*

Sec. **136**. After the action has been set down for trial, any party may apply to the judge or surrogate, on notice to any other party appearing, for an order fixing the time and place of trial. Time and place of trial.

Sec. **137**. The judge or surrogate may order such trial to take place before himself or before the judge or any surrogate. Judge or surrogate may order.

Sec. **138**. Where the trial is to be had in any town or place other than that in which the pleadings are filed, it shall be the duty of the party who obtains the order fixing the place of trial to deliver to the registrar or deputy registrar with whom the pleadings are filed, a sufficient time before the day fixed for hearing, a *præcipe* requiring him to transmit to the registrar or deputy registrar nearest the place where the trial is to be had, the pleadings and such other papers as may be specified in the *præcipe*, and at the same time to deposit with him a sufficient sum to cover the expense of transmitting and retransmiting such pleadings and papers, and thereupon it shall be the duty of the registrar or deputy registrar forthwith to transmit the pleadings and such other papers as may be specified accordingly. Where trial is to be had in place other than that in which pleadings are filed.

Sec. **139**. At the trial of a contested action the plaintiff shall in general begin; but if the burden of proof lies on the defendant, the judge or surrogate may direct the defendant to begin. Who shall begin.

Sec. **140**. If there are several plaintiffs or several defendants, the judge or surrogate may direct which plaintiff or which defendant shall begin. If several plaintiffs or defendants.

Sec. **141**. The party beginning shall first address the court, and then produce his witnesses, if any. The other party or parties shall then address the court, and produce their witnesses, if any, in such order as the judge or surrogate may direct, and shall have a right to sum up their evidence. In all cases the party beginning shall have the right to reply, but shall not produce further evidence, except by permission of the judge or surrogate. Order of proceeding in the trial of an action.

Counsel

Sec. **142.** Only one counsel shall in general be heard on each side; but the judge or surrogate, if he considers that the nature of the case requires it, may allow two counsel to be heard on each side.

Uncontested action.

Sec. **143.** If the action is uncontested, the judge or surrogate may, if he thinks fit, give judgment on the evidence adduced by the plaintiff.

XXXII.—*References.*

Assessment of damages, when and to whom referred.

Sec. **144.** The judge or surrogate may, if he thinks fit, refer the assessment of damages and the taking of any account to the registrar or deputy registrar either alone, or assisted by one or more merchants as assessors.

Rules of evidence in case of reference.

Sec. **145.** The rules as to evidence, and as to the trial, shall apply, *mutatis mutandis*, to a reference to the registrar or deputy registrar, and the registrar or deputy registrar may adjourn the proceedings from time to time, and from place to place, if he shall think necessary.

Rules of practice of Supreme Court of Ontario to be observed.

Sec. **146.** The practice to be observed on references shall be the same as that prescribed by the rules of practice of the Supreme Court of Judicature for Ontario, for the regulation of references before the Master in Ordinary of the Supreme Court.

Counsel fees on reference.

Sec. **147.** Counsel may attend the hearing of any reference, but the costs so incurred shall not be allowed on taxation unless the registrar or deputy registrar shall certify that the attendance of counsel was necessary.

Report in cases of reference.

Sec. **148.** When a reference has been heard, the registrar or deputy registrar shall draw up a report in writing of the result, showing the amount, if any, found due, and to whom, together with any further particulars that may be necessary. A form of the report will be found in schedule A hereto, No. 30.

Where registrar or deputy registrar is directed to appoint money to be paid.

Sec. **149.** Where the registrar or deputy registrar is directed to appoint money to be paid at some time and place, he is to appoint the same to be paid into some incorporated bank at its head office, or at some branch or agency office of such bank in Ontario to the joint credit of the party to whom the same is made payable, and of the registrar or deputy registrar of the court; the party to whom the same is made payable to name the bank into which he desires the same to be paid, and the registrar or deputy registrar to name the place for such payment.

Where money is paid into bank in pursuance of appointment.

Sec. **150.** Where money is paid into a bank in pursuance of such appointment the party paying may pay the same either to the credit of the party to whom the same is made payable, or to the joint credit of the party and the registrar or deputy registrar, and if the same be paid to the sole credit of the party, such party shall be entitled to receive the same without an order.

Where default is made in payment.

Sec. **151.** Where default is made in the payment of money appointed to be paid into a bank, the certificate of the cashier, manager or agent of the bank where the same is made payable, or of the like bank officer shall be sufficient evidence of default.

Sec. **152.** When the report is ready, notice shall be sent to the parties, and either party may thereupon take up and file the report. **Notice of report being ready.**

Sec. **153.** Within *two weeks* from the filing of the registrar's or deputy registrar's report, either party may file a notice of motion to vary the report, specifying the items objected to. **Notice of motion to vary report.**

Sec. **154.** At the hearing of the motion the judge or surrogate may make such order thereon as to him shall seem fit, or may remit the matter to the registrar or deputy registrar for further inquiry or report. **Hearing of motion to vary.**

Sec. **155.** If no notice of motion to vary the report is filed within *two weeks* from filing the registrar's or deputy registrar's report, the report shall stand confirmed. **When report shall stand confirmed.**

Sec. **156.** The registrar or deputy registrar is to enter in the cause book from time to time the proceedings, taken before him, and the directions he gives in relation to the prosecution of the reference or otherwise. **Proceedings on reference to be entered in cause book.**

XXXIII.—*Costs.*

Sec. **157.** In general costs shall abide the event; but the judge or surrogate may in any case make such order as to the costs as to him shall seem fit. **To abide the event.**

Sec. **158.** The judge or surrogate may direct payment of a lump sum in lieu of taxed costs. **Lump sum.**

Sec. **159.** If any plaintiff (other than a seaman suing for his wages or for the loss of his clothes and effects in a collision), or any defendant making a counterclaim is not resident in the Province of Ontario, the judge or surrogate may, on the application of the adverse party, order him to give bail for costs. **Security for costs.**

Sec. **160.** A party claiming an excessive amount, either by way of claim, or of set-off or counterclaim, may be condemned in all costs and damages thereby occasioned. **Party claiming an excessive amount.**

Sec. **161.** If a tender is rejected, but is afterwards accepted, or is held by the judge or surrogate to be sufficient, the party rejecting the tender shall, unless the judge or surrogate shall otherwise order, be condemned in the costs incurred after tender made. **Tender rejected but afterwards accepted.**

Sec. **162.** A party, who has not admitted any fact which in the opinion of the judge or surrogate he ought to have admitted, may be condemned in all costs occasioned by the non-admission. **Party not admitting fact.**

Sec. **163.** Any party pleading at unnecessary length or taking any unnecessary proceeding in an action may be condemned in all costs thereby occasioned. **Pleading at unnecessary length.**

XXXIV.—*Taxation of Costs.*

Bill of costs must be filed appointment and notice.

Sec. **164**. A party desiring to have a bill of costs taxed shall file the bill, and shall procure an appointment from the registrar or deputy registrar and shall serve the opposite party or parties with notice of the time at which the taxation will take place.

Practice in Supreme Court of Ontario.

Sec. **165**. The practice upon the taxation of costs shall be regulated, subject to the provisions of these rules, by the rules and practice in force in the Supreme Court of Judicature for Ontario.

Either party present.

Sec. **166**. At the time appointed, if either party is present the taxation shall be proceeded with.

Review within one week.

Sec. **167**. Within *one week* from the completion of the taxation, application may be made to the judge or surrogate to review the taxation.

Who may tax costs: review of taxation.

Appeal from taxation.

Sec. **168**. Costs may be taxed either by the judge, or a surrogate or by the registrar or a deputy registrar, and as well between solicitor and client, as between party and party, and upon any applieation to a surrogate to review the taxation of a deputy registrar, he may refer the matter to the registrar. Either party may appeal from the taxation of the registrar to the judge.

Costs on reduction of bill.

Sec. **169**. If in a taxation between solicitor and client more than *one sixth* of the bill is struck off, the solicitor shall pay all the costs attending the taxation.

Certificate and order for payment of costs.

Sec. **170**. When a bill of costs has been taxed by the registrar or deputy registrar he shall certify at the foot of the bill the amount at which he has taxed it, and the solicitor may then if necessary apply to the judge or surrogate for an order for the payment thereof.

XXXV.—*Appraisement and Sale, &c.*

Property under arrest may be ordered to be sold by auction or otherwise, notice to be given.

Sec. **171**. The judge or surrogate may, either before or after final judgment, order any property under the arrest of the court to be appraised, or to be sold with or without appraisement, and either by public auction or by private contract and may direct what notice or notices by advertisement or otherwise shall be given or may dispense with the same.

Property deteriorating.

Sec. **172**. If the property is deteriorating in value, the judge or surrogate may order it to be sold forthwith.

Property of small value.

Sec. **173**. If the property to be sold is of small value, the judge or surrogate may, if he thinks fit, order it to be sold without a commission of sale being issued.

Removal of property under arrest.

Sec. **174**. The judge or surrogate may, either before or after final judgment order any property under arrest of the court to be removed, or any cargo under arrest on board ship to be discharged.

Appraisement, sale

Sec. **175**. The appraisement, sale and removal of property, and the discharge of cargo, shall be effected under the authority of a commission addressed to the marshal or to a deputy marshal. Forms of commissions of appraisement, sale, appraisement and sale, removal, and discharge of cargo, will be found in schedule A hereto, Nos. 31 to 35.

and removal, how effected.

Sec. **176**. Every commission for the appraisement or sale of property under the decree of the court shall, unless the judge or surrogate otherwise order, be executed by the marshal or deputy marshal, or his substitutes.

Commision, by whom executed.

Sec. **177**. The commission shall, as soon as possible after its execution, be filed by the marshal or deputy marshal with a return setting forth the manner in which it has been executed.

Commission to be filed with a return.

Sec. **178**. At the request of the purchaser the marshal or deputy marshal shall execute a bill of sale of any ship sold by him; such bill of sale to be prepared at the cost of the purchaser and tendered for execution to the marshal or deputy marshal; a copy of the decree or order for sale, authenticated by the seal of the court shall be attached to such bill of sale. A form of bill of sale will be found in schedule A hereto, No. 36.

Bills of sale, by whom executed; provisions respecting the same.

Sec. **179**. As soon as possible after the execution of a commission of sale, the marshal or deputy marshal shall pay into court the gross proceeds of the sale, and shall with the commission file his accounts and vouchers in support thereof.

Payment of proceeds into court.

Sec. **180**. The registrar or deputy registrar shall tax the marshal's or deputy marshal's account, and shall report the amount at which he considers it should be allowed; and any party who is interested in the proceeds may be heard before the registrar or deputy registrar on the taxation.

Marshal's or deputy marshal's account to be taxed.

Sec. **181**. Application may be made to the judge or surrogate on motion to review the registrar's or deputy registrar's taxation under the next preceding section.

Review of such taxation.

Sec. **182**. The judge or surrogate may, if he thinks fit, order any property under the arrest of the court to be inspected. A form of order for inspection will be found in schedule A hereto, No. 37.

Inspection of property under arrest.

Sec. **183**. No order for advertising a notice of the action and intended sale in an action *in rem*, by default, shall be made unless upon the application for such order it is made to appear to the satisfaction of the judge for surrogate as the case may be;—
(a)

Order for advertising notice, &c., in an action *in rem*, when necessary.

(*a*.) That no owner or mortgagee of the property proceeded against resides in Canada: or—

Owner non-resident.

(*b*.) That the whereabouts of none of the owners or mortgagees in Canada can be ascertained after reasonable efforts in that behalf; or—

Whereabouts of owner unknown.

(*c*.) That the institution of the action has come to the knowledge of the owners or some of them, if in Canada,—or to the knowledge of the agent in Canada of the owners or some of

Knowledge of the institution of the action.

Notice of sale - practice Williams & Bruce p 205. Rules 18, 19 in High Ct Admiralty Eng. Coote page 126 & 191.

them, and that the institution of the action has come to the knowledge of at least one of the mortgagees under each mortgage upon the property registered in Canada, or to the knowledge of his agent, if any, in Canada.

Order for sale in an action *in rem* when made.

Sec. **184**. No order for the sale of the property proceeded against in an action *in rem*, whether by default or otherwise, shall be made, unless upon the application for such order it is made to appear to the satisfaction of the judge or surrogate as the case may be;—

Knowledge to a mortgagee or his agent.

(*a*.) That the institution of the action has come to the knowledge of at least one of the mortgagees under each mortgage upon the property registered in Canada, or to the knowledge of his agent, if any, in Canada; or—

Whereabouts of mortgagee unknown.

(*b*.) That the whereabouts of none of the mortgagees in Canada can be ascertained after reasonable efforts in that behalf.

XXXVI.—*Discontinuance.*

Discontinuance by filing notice; costs in such case.

Notice to prejudice other parties.

Sec. **185**. The plaintiff may, at any time, discontinue his action by filing a notice to that effect, and the defendant shall thereupon be entitled to have judgment entered for his costs of action on filing a notice to enter the same. The discontinuance of an action by the plaintiff shall not prejudice any action consolidated therewith or any counter-claim previously set up by the defendant. Forms of notice of discontinuance and of notice to enter judgment for costs will be found in schedule A hereto, Nos. 38 and 39.

XXXVII.—*Consent.*

Consent in writing an order of court.

Sec. **186**. Any consent in writing signed by the parties may, by permission of the registrar, or deputy registrar, be filed, and shall thereupon become an order of court.

XXXVIII.—*Notice of Appeal.*

Fifteen days notice of intention to appeal.

Rules of Supreme Court of Canada to govern.

Sec. **187**. A party intending to appeal from a decision of the court to the Supreme Court of Canada must give notice of his intention to appeal to the opposite party within *fifteen days* from the time of the pronouncing of the decision appealed from, and otherwise the appeal shall be governed by the rules of the Supreme Court of Canada aforesaid. A form of notice of appeal will be found in schedule A hereto, No. 40.

XXXIX.—*Payment of Money into and out of Court.*

Canadian Bank of Commerce.

Sec. **188**. A person desiring to pay money into court shall pay the same into the Canadian Bank of Commerce at Toronto or at some branch or agency thereof or as mentioned in the next following section, and in no other way.

Branch banks or agency offices.

Sec. **189**. Money required to be paid into court in any of the following places (so long as the Canadian Bank of Commerce shall have no branch office thereat), shall be paid into the branch or agency office of the bank set opposite the said places respectively:

At Cornwall - - -	Bank of Montreal.
Kingston - -	Bank of Montreal.
Owen Sound - -	Merchants Bank.
Picton - - -	Bank of Montreal.
Port Arthur - -	Ontario Bank.

Sec. **190**. The person paying money into court shall first obtain from the registrar or deputy registrar a direction to the bank to receive the money. **Direction to the bank.**

Sec. **191**. The person applying for the direction is to file a *præcipe* therefor and is to leave with the officer issuing the direction the judgment, order, writ or pleading, or copy thereof, under which the money is payable. And in case the direction is obtained elsewhere than in Toronto he shall also leave the necessary postage for the transmission of the document to the registrar and a further copy of the pleading for transmission. **Person applying for the direction is to file a præcipe therefor.**

Sec. **192**. When the direction is issued elsewhere than in Toronto the officer issuing the same shall forthwith transmit to the registrar by post the *præcipe* for such direction together with the papers left on the application therefor. **Direction issued elsewhere than in Toronto.**

Sec. **193**. A person paying money into court elsewhere than in Toronto shall be entitled to credit therefor as of the date on which the same was deposited in the bank, but the party entitled thereto shall not be entitled to receive bank interest thereon until the money shall have been received by the Canadian Bank of Commerce at Toronto. **When credit shall be given and when interest shall commence.**

Sec. **194**. The bank on receiving money to the credit of any action or matter is to give a receipt therefor in duplicate, and one copy shall be delivered to the party making the deposit, and the other shall be posted or delivered the same day to the registrar. **Bank to give receipt in duplicate.**

Sec. **195**. When a bank receipt for the amount shall be filed, the payment into court shall be deemed to be complete. **When payment deemed complete.**

Sec. **196**. Money shall be paid out of court upon the cheque of the judge or surrogate, countersigned by the registrar and not otherwise. **Money how paid out of court.**

Sec. **197**. The person entitled to the money shall produce to and leave with the registrar the order and a copy thereof entitling such person to the money. **Production of order and copy.**

Sec. **198**. The registrar after satisfying himself that no *caveat* against the payment of the money has been entered, or if entered that it has been set aside or withdrawn, shall countersign the order thus—" No caveat entered against payment of this money —registrar," and shall re-deliver the order to the person entitled thereto after making the necessary entries in his books respecting the same. **Registrar shall countersign order if no caveat has been entered.**

Sec. **199**. Bail for latent demands shall not, unless the judge or surrogate shall otherwise order, be required on the payment of money out of court. **Bail for latent demands.**

XL.—*Account Books.*

Registrar shall keep books of account.

Sec. **200**. The registrar shall keep such books of account and otherwise relating to money in court or invested under the authority of the court as the judge may from time to time think necessary to ensure safety and accuracy and ready reference.

Inspection of books and certificate.

Sec. **201**. The books so kept shall be open to inspection, and the registrar shall give a certificate of the state of any account or an extract therefrom at the desire of any party interested or his solicitor.

XLI.—*Caveats.*

To prevent the arrest of property, notice may be filed and *caveat* entered.

Sec. **202**. Any person desiring to prevent the arrest of any property may file a notice, undertaking within *three days* after being required to do so, to give bail to any action or counterclaim that may have been, or may be, brought against the property, and thereupon the registrar or deputy registrar shall enter a *caveat* in the "*caveat* warrant book" hereinafter mentioned. Forms of notice and of *caveat* warrant will be found in schedule A hereto, Nos. 41 and 42.

To prevent release of property under arrest.

Sec. **203**. Any person desiring to prevent the release of any property under arrest, shall file a notice, and thereupon the registrar or deputy registrar shall enter a *caveat* in the "*caveat* release book" hereinafter mentioned. Forms of notice and of *caveat* release will be found in schedule A hereto, Nos. 43 and 44.

To prevent payment of money out of court.

Sec. **204**. Any person desiring to prevent the payment of money out of court shall file a notice, and thereupon the registrar shall enter a *caveat* in the "*caveat* payment book" hereinafter mentioned. Forms of notice and of *caveat* payment will be found in schedule A hereto, Nos. 45 and 46.

If person entering *caveat* is not a party.

Sec. **205**. If the person entering a *caveat* is not a party to the action, the notice shall state his name and address, and an address within three miles of the registry at which it shall be sufficient to leave all documents required to be served upon him.

Entry of *caveat* warrant shall not prevent issue of warrant.

Sec. **206**. The entry of a *caveat* warrant shall not prevent the issue of a warrant, but a party at whose instance a warrant shall be issued for the arrest of any property in respect of which there is a *caveat* warrant outstanding, shall be condemned in all costs and damages occasioned thereby, unless he shall show to the satisfaction of the judge or surrogate good and sufficient reason to the contrary.

Liability of party entering *caveat* release or *caveat* payment.

Sec. **207**. The party at whose instance a *caveat* release or *caveat* payment is entered, shall be condemned in all costs and damages occasioned thereby, unless he shall show to the satisfaction of the judge or surrogate good and sufficient reason to the contrary.

If *caveat* not entered in office where writ issued.

Sec. **208**. If the *caveat* has not been entered in the office where the writ is issued, the registrar or any deputy registrar with whom a *caveat* has been entered, shall on the plaintiff's application transmit to the registrar or deputy registrar at whose office the writ is issued, a certified copy of the undertaking upon which the *caveat* was entered.

Sec. **209**. A *caveat* shall not remain in force for more than *six months* from the date of entering the same. **Expiry of *caveat.***

Sec. **210**. A *caveat* may at any time be withdrawn by the person at whose instance it has been entered, on his filing a notice withdrawing it. A form of notice of withdrawal will be found in schedule A hereto, No. 47. **Withdrawal of *caveat.***

Sec. **211**. The judge or surrogate may overrule any *caveat*. **Overruling *caveat.***

Sec. **212**. Application may be made in chambers to overrule any *caveat*. **Application in chambers.**

XLII.—*Subpœnas.*

Sec. **213**. Any party desiring to compel the attendance of a witness shall serve him with a *subpœna*, which shall be prepared by the party and issued under the seal of the court. Forms of *subpœnas* will be found in schedule A hereto, Nos. 48 and 49. **Attendance of witnesses.**

Sec. **214**. A *subpœna* may contain the names of any number of witnesses, or may be issued with the names of the witnesses in blank. **Any number of witnesses or in blank.**

Sec. **215**. Service of the *subpœna* must be personal, and may be made by the party or his agent, and shall be proved by affidavit. **Personal service.**

XLIII.—*Orders for payment.*

Sec. **216**. On application by a party to whom any sum has been found due, the judge or surrogate may order payment to be made out of any money in court applicable for the purpose. **Payment out of money in court.**

If there is no such money in court, or if it is insufficient, the judge or surrogate may order that the party liable shall pay the sum found due, or the balance thereof, as the case may be, within such time as to the judge or surrogate shall seem fit. The party to whom the sum is due may then obtain from the registry and serve upon the party liable an order for payment under seal of the court. A form of order for payment will be found in schedule A hereto, No. 50. **Payment when no money in court or the amount is insufficient.**

XLIV.—*Attachments.*

Sec. **217**. If any person disobeys an order of the court, or commits a contempt of court, the judge or surrogate may order him to be attached. A form of such attachment will be found in schedule A hereto, No. 51. **Contempt of court.**

Sec. **218**. The person attached shall without delay be brought before the judge or surrogate, and if he persists in his disobedience or contempt, the judge or surrogate may order him to be committed. Forms of order for committal and of committal will be found in schedule A hereto, Nos. 52 and 53. **Proceedings when person attached for disobedience or contempt.**

The order for committal shall be executed by the marshal or deputy marshal. **Order for committal.**

XLV.—*Amending Decree or Order.*

Application to amend, &c., may be made in Chambers.

Sec. **219.** An application to amend an order, which has not been drawn up in conformity with the judgment pronounced, so as to make the same conformable thereto, and an application to correct any clerical mistake in an order or an error arising from an accidental slip or omission, may be made in chambers, and the judge or surrogate may grant the same if under all circumstances he sees fit.

XLVI.—*Execution.*

Enforcement of decree or or order.

Sec. **220.** Any decree or order of the court may be enforced in the same manner as a decree or order of the Supreme Court of Judicature for the Province of Ontario may be enforced. A form of writ of execution (*Fiere Facias*) will be found in schedule A hereto, No. 54.

Form of writ of execution.

XLVII.—*Instruments, &c.*

Warrant, release, execution, &c., to be prepared in registry.

Sec. **221.** Every warrant, release, execution, commission, attachment, and other instrument to be executed by any officer of, or commissioner acting under the authority of the court, shall be prepared in the registry and signed by the registrar or deputy registrar, and shall be issued under the seal of the court.

When deemed to be issued.

Sec. **222.** Every document issued under the seal of the court shall bear date on the day of sealing, and shall be deemed to be issued at the time of the sealing thereof.

Time for service, six months.

Sec. **223.** Every document requiring to be served shall be served within *six months* from the date thereof, otherwise the service shall not be valid.

Instrument to be executed shall be left with marshal or deputy.

Sec. **224.** Every instrument to be executed by the marshal or deputy marshal shall be left with the marshal or deputy marshal by the party at whose instance it is issued, with written instructions for the execution thereof.

XLVIII.—*Notices from the Registry.*

Notice from registry may be served by post.

Sec. **225.** Any notice from the registry may be either left at, or sent by post, by registered letter to, the address for service of the party to whom notice is to be given, and the day next after the day on which the notice is so posted shall be considered as the day of service thereof, and the posting thereof as aforesaid shall be a sufficient service.

XLIX.—*Filing.*

Mode of filing documents.

Sec. **226.** Documents shall be filed by leaving the same in the registry, with a *minute* stating the nature of the document, and the date of filing it. A form of *minute* on filing any document will be found in schedule A. hereto, No. 55.

One *minute* sufficient.

Sec. **227.** Any number of documents in the same action may be filed with one and the same *minute*.

Sec. **228**. No document, except preliminary acts, bail bonds, documents issued from the registry, and minutes shall be filed without a certificate indorsed thereon, signed by the party filing the same, that a copy thereof has been served npon the adverse party, if any. **Indorsement of certificate, when required.**

L.—*Time.*

Sec. **229**. If the time for doing any act or taking any proceeding in an action expires on a Sunday, or on any other day on which the registry is closed, and by reason thereof, such act or proceeding cannot be done or taken on that day, it may be done or taken on the next day on which the registry is open. **Expiry of time on Sunday, &c.**

Sec. **230**. Where, by these rules or by any order made under them, any act or proceeding is ordered or allowed to be done within or after the expiration of a time limited from or after any date or event, such time, if not limited by hours, shall not include the day of such date or of the happening of such event, but shall commence on the next following day. **When time for doing any act shall commence.**

Sec. **231**. The judge or surrogate may on the application of either party, enlarge or abridge the time prescribed by these rules or forms or by any order made under them for doing any act or taking any proceeding, upon such terms as to him shall seem fit, and any such enlargement may be ordered although the application for the same is not made until after the expiration of the time prescribed **Time may be enlarged or abridged.**

LI.—*Sittings of the Court.*

Sec. **232**. The judge or surrogate shall appoint proper and convenient times for sittings in court and in chambers, and may adjourn the proceedings from time to time and from place to place as to him shall seem fit. **Sittings and adjournments**

LII.—*Office Hours.*

Sec. **233**. The offices of the court shall be open on every day in the year except on Sundays, New Year's day, Good Friday, Easter Monday, Christmas day, and the days appointed for the celebration of the birthday of Her Majesty and Her Royal successors, and any day appointed by proclamation for a general fast or thanksgiving. ***Dies non.***

LIII..—*Registrar.*

Sec. **234**. The registrar shall attend all sittings of the court held in Toronto and also before the judge in chambers and shall make minutes of every act of the court or decree and enter the same in a proper book to be kept for the purpose, which is to form a record of the court, and shall do and perform all the other duties imposed upon him by these or any future rules, and by the practice of the court. If from illness or any other sufficient cause he should be unable to perform his duty, he may with the consent of the judge, or the judge himself may, appoint some other competent person to act as registrar on those occasions. He is pro- **Registrar shall attend all sittings of the courts in Toronto and in chambers.** **Absence of registrar provided for.**

Shall not act as solicitor, &c.

hibited from acting as either solicitor or advocate in any suit, matter or proceeding in the court.

LIV.—*Deputy Registrar.*

Deputy registrar shall attend all sittings of the court in the place where he keeps his office and in chambers.

Absence of deputy registrar provided for.

Shall not act as solicitor, &c.

Sec. **235**. The deputy registrar shall attend all sittings of the court held in the place where he keeps his office and also in chambers, before the surrogate residing nearest such place, and shall make minutes of every act of the court or decree and enter the same in a proper book to be kept for the purpose which is to form a record of the court; and shall do and perform all the other duties imposed upon him by these or any future rules, and by the practice of the court. If from illness or any other sufficient cause he should be unable to perform his duty, he may with the consent of the surrogate; or the surrogate himself may, appoint some other competent person to act as deputy registrar on those occasions. He is prohibited from acting as either solicitor or advocate in any suit, matter or proceeding in court.

LV.—*Marshal.*

Marshal shall atten judge, execute writs, &c., and make due return thereof.

Sec. **236**. The marshal shall attend the judge in court on all court days. He is to execute all such writs, warrants, decrees, monitions and instruments and orders as shall be issued from the court, and be directed to him, and he is to make due return thereof and to do and perform all other duties imposed on him by these or any future rules, or by the practice of the court.

LVI.—*Deputy Marshal.*

Deputy marshal shall attend sittings and execute warrants.

Shall make due return.

Sec. **237**. The deputy marshal shall attend all sittings of the court on court days held in the place where he keeps his office. He is to execute all such warrants, decrees, monitions and instruments and orders as shall be issued from the court and be directed to him, and he is to make due return thereof and to do and perform all other duties imposed on him by these or any future rules, or by the practice of the court.

In case of distance or other cause.

Sec. **238**. Whenever, by reason of distance or other sufficient cause, the marshal or deputy marshal can not conveniently execute any instrument in person, he shall employ some competent person as his officer to execute the same.

LVII.—*Security of Marshal and Deputy Marshal.*

Judge or surrogate shall fix security.

Limit of time and the mode and terms relating to security to be given by marshals or deputy marshals.

Form of duplicate covenant.

Sec. **239**. The judge or surrogate shall fix and determine the amount of security to be given by the marshal and each deputy marshal. Every marshal and deputy marshal shall, before he is sworn into office, and within *one month* after his appointment; or in the case of the marshal or deputy marshals already appointed within one month after notice to that effect from the judge or surrogate, execute and enter into a joint and several covenant in duplicate with two or more sureties of such amounts respectively as shall have been fixed by the judge or surrogate in that behalf as aforesaid for the due performance of the duties of his office, and the proper accounting for all moneys coming in or passing through his hands. Such duplicate covenant shall be in the form No. 56 of schedule A hereto, or to the like effect; and to each of the duplicate covenants respectively shall be attached an affidavit made by each of the covenantors therein named respectively in the form provided by No. 57 of schedule A hereto, or to the like effect. **Affidavit of justification.**

Sec. **240**. The said duplicate covenants, with the affidavits thereto attached, shall within the periods hereinbefore limited respectively be filed with the registrar or deputy registrar of the said court; and the same shall be brought before the judge or surrogate by the said registrar or deputy registrar for approval; and when the same shall be indorsed by the said judge or surrogate as approved, one duplicate thereof shall be transmitted to the Minister of Justice at Ottawa for his approval. And in case the said Minister of Justice shall disapprove of the same he may forthwith give notice to the marshal or deputy marshal of such disapproval and in such case the marshal or deputy marshal shall within one month thereafter furnish another covenant in lieu of the covenant so disapproved of as aforesaid to the satisfaction of the said judge or surrogate and the Minister of Justice. **The duplicate covenants and affidavits attached thereto shall be filed and submitted for approval, and transmitted to the Minister of Justice.**

Sec. **241**. The sureties named in any covenant so disapproved of as aforesaid shall not be discharged from liability by such disapproval, but shall be and continue liable for any defaults or misfeasances made, done or committed previous to the approval by the Minister of Justice of any securities that may be furnished in lieu of the same. **Sureties disapproved. To continue liable.**

Sec. **242**. The judge or surrogate may at any time require the marshal or any deputy marshal to renew his covenants or securities or to furnish others in lieu of the same. as to the judge or surrogate may appear expedient for the protection of the interests of the Crown or of parties to legal proceedings, which new or substituted covenants or securities the marshal or any deputy marshal shall be bound to furnish in the same manner and subject to the same provisions as hereinbefore provided, within three months after notice from the judge or surrogate in that behalf. **Renewal or substitution of covenants may be required.**

Sec. **243**. Every renewed or substituted covenant or security shall be in the same form and executed and accompanied by the same formalities and affidavits, and subject to the same approval as the original covenant or security. **Form of renewed or substituted covenant.**

Sec. **244**. In case a new security is given or substituted as aforesaid the former sureties shall only be liable for or on account of defaults or misfeasances suffered or committed by the marshal or deputy marshal previous to the perfecting of the new security and the approval thereof by the judge or surrogate and the Minister of Justice; and not as to any subsequent default or misfeasance. **Liability of former sureties.**

Sec. **245**. In case of the default by the marshal or any deputy marshal to furnish such security as aforesaid within the time above limited it shall be the duty of the judge or surrogate to report the fact forthwith to the Minister of Justice. **Default in furnishing security.**

LVIII.—*Seal of the Court.*

Judge shall cause design to be made.

Sec. **246.** The judge shall cause a design for the seal of the conrt to be made. A seal shall be kept and used by the registrar and by each deputy registrar.

All instruments, &c., to be sealed.

Sec. **247.** All instruments, orders and decrees of court, office copies and other documents issued by the registrar or deputy registrar shall be sealed with the seal of the court.

LXI.—*Teste.*

Monitions, &c.

Sealing and signing.

Sec. **248.** Monitions, warrants, attachments, subpœnas, writs, and other instruments and orders of the court running in the name of Her Majesty the Queen, shall be given under the seal of the court, and signed by the registrar or deputy registrar.

LX.—*Records of the Court.*

Requisites and mode of keeping the *minute* book.

Sec. **249.** There shall be kept in the registry a book, to be called the "*minute* book," in which the registrar or deputy registrar shall enter in order of date, under the head of each action, and on a page numbered with the number of the action, a record of the commencement of the action, of all appearances entered, all document issued or filed, all acts done, and all orders and decrees of the court, whether made by the judge or surrogate, or by the registrar or deputy registrar, or by consent of the parties in the action. Forms of minute of order of court, of minute on examination of witnesses, of minute of decree, and of minutes in an action for damage by collision, will be found in schedule A hereto, Nos. 58 to 61.

Other books to be kept in registry.

Sec. **250.** There shall be kept in the registry a "*caveat* warrant book," a "*caveat* release book," and a "*caveat* payment book," in which all such *caveats* respectively and the withdrawal thereof shall be entered by the registrar or deputy registrar.

Inspection of books.

Sec. **251.** Any person may inspect the *minute* and *caveat* books, on payment of the proper fees.

LXI.—*Copies.*

Office copies may be obtained.

Sec. **252.** Any person entitled to inspect any document in an action shall, on payment of the proper charges for the same, be entitled to an office copy thereof under seal of the court.

LXII.—*Forms.*

Forms of Supreme Court of Ontario, how far applicable.

Sec. **253.** The forms hereto annexed shall be followed as nearly as the circumstances of the case will allow and in cases not provided for the forms in use in actions in the Supreme Court of Judicature for the Province of Ontario, *mutatis mutandis*, may be followed.

LXIII.—*Tariff of Fees.*

Fees in schedule B.

Sec. **254.** The fees to be paid to the practitioners, officers and witnesses in causes in the court shall be as set forth in the Tariff of Fees in schedule B hereto.

Sec. **255.** The fees and disbursements set forth in the said Tariff of Fees may be charged in respect of the services therein enumerated subject to the following rules. **Fees subject to following rules.**

Sec. **256.** When the fee is per folio, the folio shall be counted at the rate of 100 words, and every numeral, whether contained in columns or otherwise written, shall be counted and charged for as a word. **Folio.**

Sec. **257.** When the sum in dispute does not exceed $200 or the value of the *res* does not exceed $400, one-half only of the fees set forth in the said Tariff of Fees shall be charged and allowed; and if the judge or surrogate shall so order and direct the government fees in such cases may likewise be reduced to one half. This section is subject to the provisions of Chapter 75 of the Revised Statutes of Canada, intituled "The Inland Waters Seamen's Act." **Half fees in certain cases.**

Sec. **258.** When costs are awarded to a plaintiff, the expression "sum in dispute" shall mean the sum recovered by him in addition to the sum, if any, counterclaimed from him by the defendant; and where "costs" are awarded to a defendant, it shall mean the sum claimed from him in addition to the sum, if any, recovered by him. **"Sums in dispute." "Costs."**

Sec. **259.** Two or more persons having claims against the same property for wages or for necessaries may join against the same property in one writ, and unless the sum or sums adjudged to the claimant or claimants in a writ in an action of wages or of necessaries amount to the sum of one hundred dollars at least, no costs shall be allowed to the claimant or claimants, as the case may be, unless under all the circumstances the judge or surrogate thinks proper to allow a sum in gross not exceeding ten dollars in lieu of all costs. **When two or more persons have claims against the same property for wages or necessaries amounting to $100.**

This section does not authorize the joining in one writ a claim for wages and a claim for necessaries. **Non-joinder.**

Sec. **260.** The judge or surrogate may in any action order that half fees only shall be allowed, including the Government fees. **Half fees in any action.**

Sec. **261.** Bonds executed under an order for security for costs are to be given to the registrar or deputy registrar from whose office the writ issued; all the defendants are to be included in the same bond and the penal sum to be inserted therein is to be fixed upon the application for security, by the judge or surrogate who makes the order. **Bonds for security for costs.**

LXIV.—*Miscellaneous.*

Sec. **262.** In all cases where a reference to the registrar or deputy registrar may be directed the court may dispose of such matters itself if it thinks fit, and may direct the proceedings to be taken in full court or in chambers as it finds expedient. **The court may itself dispose of matters suitable for reference.**

Sec. **263.** Where on a proceeding before an officer of the court pleadings or other documents filed with another officer of **Where documents filed** with another officer are required, certificate required mode and expense of transmission.

the court are required, the officer with whom the pleading or other documents are filed is upon production of a certificate signed by the officer requiring the pleadings or other documents, that the same are required for some proceedings before him, to transmit the pleadings or other documents mentioned in the certificate, but if they are to be sent by parcel post or by express, before they are sent the party requiring their transmission is to deposit a sufficient sum to cover the expense of transmission and of re-transmission to the office from which they are sent.

Re-transmission of document.

Sec. **264**. As soon as the purpose for which any such documents are required is completed the officer to whom they have been sent is to retransmit them to the office from which they were sent.

"The solicitor's and agent's book."

Sec. **265**. The registrar and each deputy registrar shall keep in his office a book to be called "the solicitor's and agent's book," in which each solicitor, residing elsewhere than in the place where such registrar's or deputy registrar's office may be, is to specify the name of an agent being a person entitled to act as a solicitor or attorney-at-law in Ontario, and having an office in such place, upon whom pleadings, writs, notices, orders, appointments, warrants and other documents and communications connected with any cause or matter in the office of such registrar or deputy registrar, as the case may be, may be served.

LXV.—*Repealing Clause.*

May 1, 1889.

Sec. **266**. From and after the first day of May, 1889, except in regard to actions commenced before that day, the rules and regulations, together with all forms thereto annexed, and all tables of fees now in force in this court shall be repealed.

LXVI.—*Commencement of Rules.*

Rules, etc., in operation.

Sec. **267**. These rules together with the following forms and tables of fees shall come into operation on the first day of May, 1889, and shall apply to all actions commenced on or after that day. Actions commenced before that day may, by consent of the parties, and with the permission of the judge or surrogate, be continued under these rules on such terms as to the judge or surrogate shall seem fit.

Actions pending.

[Made and signed by Joseph E. McDougall, the judge of the said court, January 31st, 1889.]

SCHEDULE A.

FORMS.

No. 1.

TITLE OF ACTION IN REM. Section 4.

No. [*Here insert the number of the action.*]

A.B., Plaintiff,

against

(*a.*) The Ship
or (*b.*) The Ship and freight.
or (*c.*) The Ship her cargo and freight.
or (*if the action is against the cargo only*),
(*d.*) The cargo *ex* the Ship [*state the name of ship on board of which the cargo now is or lately was laden.*]
or (*if the action is against the proceeds realized by the sale of the Ship or cargo*),
(*e.*) The proceeds of the Ship
or (*f.*) The proceeds of the cargo *ex* the Ship
[*or as the case may be.*]

Action for [*state nature of action, whether for damage by collision, wages, bottomry, &c., as the case may be.*]

No. 2.

TITLE OF ACTION IN PERSONAM. Section 4.

No. [*Here insert the number of the action.*]

A.B., Plaintiff,

against

The owners of the Ship [*or as the case may be.*]

Action for [*state nature of action as in preceding form.*]

No. 3.

WRIT OF SUMMONS IN REM.

In the Maritime Court of Ontario.

(L.S.) [*Here insert title of action.*]

VICTORIA, by the Grace of God, of the United Kingdom of Great Britain and Ireland, Queen, Defender of the Faith.

To the owners and all others interested in the Ship.
[her cargo and freight, *&c., or as the case may be.*]

We command you that, within *one week* after the service of this writ, exclusive of the day of such service, you do cause an appearance to be entered for you in Our Maritime Court of Ontario in the above-named action; and take notice that in default of your so doing the said action may proceed, and judgment may be given in your absence.

Given at in Our said Court, under the seal thereof, this day of , 18 .

Memorandum to be subscribed on the Writ.

This writ may be served within *six months* from the date thereof, exclusive of the day of such date, but not afterwards.

The Defendant (*or* Defendants) may appear hereto by entering an appearance (*or* appearances) either personally or by solicitor at the registry of the said court situate at

---

No. 4.

Section 5.

WRIT OF SUMMONS IN PERSONAM.

In the Maritime Court of Ontario.

(L.S.) [*Here insert title of action.*]

VICTORIA, by the grace of God, &c.

To *C.D.*, of , and *E.F.*, of

We command you that, within *one week* after the service of this writ, exclusive of the day of such service, you do cause an appearance to be entered for you in our Maritime Court of Ontario, in the above-named action; and take notice that in default of your so doing the said action may proceed, and judgment may be given in your absence.

Given at in Our said Court, under the seal thereof, this day of , 18 .

Memorandum to be subscribed on the Writ.

This writ may be served within *six months* from the date thereof, exclusive of the day of such date, but not afterwards.

The Defendant (*or* Defendants) may appear hereto by entering an an appearance (*or* appearances) either personally or by solicitor at the registry of the said court situate at

---

No. 5.

Section 5.

INDORSEMENTS TO BE MADE ON THE WRIT BEFORE ISSUE THEREOF.

(1.) The Plaintiff claims [*Insert description of claim as given in Form No.* 6.]

(2.) This writ was issued by the Plaintiff in person, who resides at [*state Plaintiff's place of residence, with name of street and number of house, if any.*]

or,

This writ was issued by C.D., of [*state place of business*] solicitor for the Plaintiff.

(3.) All documents required to be served upon the said Plaintiff in the action may be left for him at [*insert address for service within three miles of the registry.*]

or,

Where the action is in the name of the Crown.

(1.) *A.B.*, etc., claims [*insert description of claim as given in Form No.* 6.]

(2.) This writ was issued by *A.B.* [*state name and address of person prosecuting in the name of the Crown, or his solicitor, or as the case may be.*]

(3.) All documents required to be served upon the Crown in this action may be left at [*insert address for service within three miles of the registry*].

No. 6.

Indorsements of Claim.

Section 5.

(1.) *Damage by collision :*

The Plaintiffs as owners of the Ship "Mary" [her cargo and freight, etc., *or as the case may be*] claim the sum of $ against the ship "Jane" for damage occasioned by a collision which took place [*state where*] on the day of ; and for costs.

(2.) *Salvage :*

The Plaintiffs, as the owners, master, and crew of the Ship "Mary," claim the sum of $ for salvage services rendered by them to the Ship "Jane" [her cargo and freight, etc., *or as the case may be*] on the day of 18 , in or near [*state where the services were rendered*]; and for costs.

(3.) *Pilotage :*

The Plaintiff claims the sum of $ for pilotage of the Ship "Jane" on the day of 18 , from [*state were pilotage commenced*] to [*state where pilotage ended*] and for costs.

(4.) *Towage :*

The Plaintiffs, as owners of the Ship "Mary," claim the sum of $ for towage services rendered by the said Ship to the Ship "Jane" [her cargo and freight, etc., *or as the case may be*], on the day of 18 , at or near [*state where the services were rendered*]; and for costs.

(5.) *Master's wages and disbursements :*

The Plaintiff claims the sum of $ for his wages and disbursements as Master of the Ship "Mary" and to have an account taken thereof; and for costs.

(6.) *Seamen's Wages.*

The Plaintiffs, as seamen on board the Ship "Mary," claim the sum of $, for wages due to them, as follows; and for costs:

to *A.B.*, the mate, $ for two month's wages from the day of to *C.D.*, able seamen, $ etc., etc.; [and the Plaintiffs claim to have an account taken thereof.]

(7.) *Necessaries, repairs, etc. :*

The plaintiffs claim the sum of $, for necessaries supplied (*or* repairs done, etc., *as the case may be*) to the Ship "Mary" at the port of on the day of ; and for costs [and the the Plaintiffs claim to have an account taken thereof].

(8.) *Possession :*

(*a*) The Plaintiff, as sole owner of the Ship "Mary," of the port of , claims possession of the said Ship.

(*b*) The Plaintiff, as owner of the 48-64th shares of the Ship "Mary" of the port of , claims possession of the said Ship as against *C.D.*, owner of the 16-64th shares of the same Ship.

(9.) *Mortgage :*

The Plaintiff, under a mortgage dated the day of , claims against the proceeds of the Ship "Mary" the sum of $, as the amount due to him for principal and interest, and for costs.

(10.) *Claims between Co-Owners :*

(*a*) The Plaintiff, as part owner of the Ship "Mary," claims against *C.D.*, part owner of the same Ship, the sum of $ as part of the earnings of the said Ship due to the Plaintiff, and for costs; and to have an account taken thereof.

Section 5. (*b.*) The Plaintiff, as owner of 24-64th shares of the Ship "Mary," being dissatisfied with the management of the said Ship by his co-owners, claims that his co-owners shall give bail in the sum of $, the value of his said shares, for the safe return of the Ship to this Province.

(11) *Bottomry*:

The Plaintiff, as assignee of a bottomry bond, dated the day of , aud granted by *C.D.*, as master of the Ship "Mary" of , to *A.B.* at the port of , claims the sum of $ against the Ship "Mary" [her cargo and freight, &c., *or as the case may be*] as the amount due to him under the said bond, and for costs.

No. 7.

Section 18.

Affidavit of Service of Writ of Summons.

In the Maritime Court of Ontario.

[*Title of action.*]

County of

I, *A.B.*, of the [*city, town, &c.*] of [*name of place*] [*calling or occupation*] make oath and say:

1. That I did on the day of 18 , serve the writ of summons herein by [*here state particularly the mode in which service was effected and whether on the owner or on the ship, cargo, or freight, &c., as the case may be*].

2. That I necessarily travelled miles to effect said service.

Sworn before me, &c. }

A Commissioner, &c.

(Signed) *A.B.*

No. 8.

Section 25.

Appearance.

(1.) *By Defendant in person.*.

In the Maritime Court of Ontario.

[*Title of action.*]

Take notice that I appear in this action.

Dated this day of 18

(Signed) *C.D.*, Defendant.

My address is

My address for service is

Section 25.

Appearance.

(2) *By Solicitor for Defendant.*

In the Maritime Court of Ontario.

[*Title of Action.*]

Take notice that I appear for *C. D.* of [*insert address of C. D.*] in this action.

Dated this day of 18

(Signed) *X. Y.*,
Solicitor for *C. D.*

My place of business is

My address for service is

No. 9.

INDORSEMENT OF SET-OFF OR COUNTERCLAIM. Section 25.

The Defendant [*or, if he be one of several Defendants*, the Defendant *C. D.*] owner of the ship "Mary" [*or, as the case may be*] claims from the Plaintiff [or claims to set-off against the Plaintiff's claim] the sum of for [*state the nature of the set-off or counterclaim and the relief or remedy required as in Form No.* 6, *mutatis mutandis*] and for costs.

No. 10.

AFFIDAVIT TO LEAD WARRANT,—GENERAL. Section 34.

In the Maritime Court of Ontario.

[*Title of Action.*]

I, *A. B.*, [*state name and address*] make oath and say that I have a claim against the Ship "Mary" for [*state nature of claim.*]

And I further make oath and say that the said claim has not been satisfied, and that the aid of this Court is required to enforce it.

On the day of 18 the said *A.B.* was duly sworn to the truth of this affidavit at } (Signed) *A.B.*

Before me,

E.F., &c.

No. 11. Section 34.

AFFIDAVIT TO LEAD WARRANT IN A CAUSE OF RESTRAINT.

In the Maritime Court of Ontario.

[*Ttle of Action.*]

I, *A.B.*, of, &c., make oath and say as follows:

1. I am the lawful owner of [*state the number of shares*] sixty-fourth shares of the or vessel belonging to the port of and the value of my said shares amounts to the sum of dollars or thereabouts.

2. The said vessel is now lying at and is in the possession or under the control of the owner of [*state number*] sixty-fourth shares thereof, and is about to be despatched by him on a voyage to against my consent.

3. I am desirous that the said vessel be restrained from proceeding until security be given to the extent of my interest therein for her safe return to the said port of and the aid and process of the Maritime Court of Ontario are necessary in that behalf.

Sworn, &c. (Signed) A. B.
the day of, &c.,

No. 12.

Section 34. **Affidavit to lead Warrant in a cause of Possession.**

In the Maritime Court of Ontario.

[*Title of Action.*]

I, *A. B.*, of, &c., make oath and say as follows:

1. I am the lawful owner of [*state the number of shares*] sixty-fourth shares of the or vessel belonging to the port of .

2. That the said vessel is now lying at and is in the possession or under the control of [*state the name, address and description of the person retaining possession and state whether he is the master or part owner, and if owner of how many shares,*] and the said refuses to deliver up the same to me, and the certificate of registry of the said vessel is also unlawfully withheld from me by the said who is now in possession thereof.

3. The aid and process of the Maritime Court of Ontario are necessary to enable me to obtain possession of the said vessel and of the certificate of registry.

Sworn, &c.

(Signed) A. B.

No. 13.

Section 39. **Warrant.**

In the Maritime Court of Ontario.

(L.S.) [*Title of Action.*]

Victoria, &c.

To the marshal and to each deputy marshal of the Maritime Court of Ontario, and to all and singular the substitutes thereof,—Greeting.

We hereby command you to arrest the ship [her cargo and freight, &c., *or as the case may be*], and to keep the same under safe arrest, until you shall receive further orders from us.

Given at in our said court, under the seal thereof, this day of 18

Warrant;
Taken out by

(Signed) E. F.,
Registrar (*or* Deputy Registrar.)

No 14.

Section 43. **Certificate of Service to be indorsed on the Warrant after Service thereof.**

This warrant was served by [*state by whom and in what mode service was effected*] on the day of 18 .

(Signed) *G H.*,
Marshal (*or* Deputy Marshal).

No. 15.

BAIL BOND. Section 48.

In the Maritime Court of Ontario.

[*Title of Action.*]

Know all men by these presents that we [*insert names, addresses, and descriptions of the sureties in full*] hereby jointly and severally submit ourselves to the jurisdiction of the said court, and consent that if the said [*insert name of party for whom bail is to be given, and state whether Plaintiff or Defendant,*] shall not pay what may be adjudged against him in the above named action, with costs [*or*, for costs, *if bail is to be given only for costs*], execution may issue against us, our heirs, executors, and administrators, goods and chattels, for a sum not exceeding [*state sum in letters*] dollars.

This Bail Bond was signed by the said
and
the sureties, the day of 18 [*or as the case may be.*] } *Signatures of sureties.*

Before me,
E. F.,
Registrar (*or* Deputy Registrar *or* a Commissioner).

No. 16. Section 49.

AFFIDAVIT OF JUSTIFICATION.

In the Maritime Court of Ontario.

[*Title of Action.*]

I, [*state name, address, and description of surety,*] one of the proposed sureties for [*state name, address, and description of person for whom bail is to be given*] make oath and say that I am worth more than the sum of [*state in letters the sum in which bail is to be given*] after the payment of all my debts.

On the day
18 , the said
was duly sworn to the truth of this affidavit at
Before me,
E. F., Registrar,
(*or* Deputy Registrar,
or Commissioner, *as the case may be.*) } *Signature of surety.*

No. 17.

RELEASE. Section 55.

In the Maritime Court of Ontario.

(L.S.) [*Title of Action.*]

VICTORIA, &c.

To the marshal and each deputy marshal of the Maritime Court of Ontario, and to all and singular the substitutes thereof,—Greeting.

Whereas by our warrant issued in the above-named action on the day of 18 , we did command you to arrest [*state name and nature of property arrested*] and to keep the same under safe arrest until you should receive further orders from us. We do hereby command you to release the said [*state name and nature of property to be released*] from the said arrest upon payment being made to you of all fees due to, and charges incurred by you in respect of the arrest and custody thereof.

Given at , in our said court, under the seal thereof, this day of 18 .

Release:
Taken out by

(Signed) *E.F.*
Registrar, (*or* Deputy Registrar.)

No. 18.

Section 69.

INTERROGATORIES.

In the Maritime Court of Ontario.

[*Title of Action.*]

Interrogatories on behalf of the Plaintiff *A.B.* [*or* Defendant *C.D.*] for the examination of the Defendants *C.D.* and *E.F.* [*or* Plaintiff *A.B.*, *or as the case may be*].

1. Did not, &c.
2. Have not, &c.

The Defendant *C.D.* is required to answer the interrogatories numbered

The Defendant *E.F.* is required to answer the interrogatories numbered

Dated the day of 18 ,

(Signed) *A.B.* [*or C.D., as the case may be*].

No. 19.

Section 69.

ANSWERS TO INTERROGATORIES.

In the Maritime Court of Ontario.

[*Title of Action.*]

The answers of the Defendant *C.D.* [*or* Plaintiff *A.B.*, *&c.*] to the interrogatories filed for his examination by the Plaintiff *A,B.* [*or* Defendant *C.D.*, *&c.*

In answer to the said interrogatories I, the above-named *C.D.* [*or A.B. &c.*], make oath and say as follows.

1.
2.

&c. &c. &c.

On the day of 18 , the said *C.D.* [*or A.B.*, *&c.*] was duly sworn to the truth of this affidavit at
Before me,
E.F., *&c.*

(Signed) *C.D.* [*or A.B.*]

No. 20.

NOTICE OF TENDER. **Section 93.**

In the Maritime Court of Ontario,

[*Title of Action.*]

Take notice that I have paid into court, and tender in satisfaction of the Plaintiff's claim [*or as the case may be*] [*if the tender is for costs also, add* including costs,] the sum of [*state sum tendered both in letters and figures, and on what terms, if any, the tender is made.*]

Dated the day of 18 .

(Signed) *C.D.*, Defendant.

No. 21.

NOTICE ACCEPTING OR REJECTING TENDER. **Section 93.**

In the Maritime Court of Ontario.

[*Title of Action.*]

Take notice that I accept [*or* reject] the tender made by the Defendant in this action,

Dated day of 18 .

(Signed) *A.B.* Plaintiff.

No. 22

INTERPRETER'S OATH. **Section 100.**

You swear that you are well acquainted with the English and languages, and that you will faithfully interpret between the court and the witnesses.

So help you God.

No 23.

APPOINTMENT TO ADMINISTER OATH IN ANY PARTICULAR PROCEEDING. **Section 103.**

In the Maritime Court of Ontario.

(L.S.)

[*Title of Action.*]

To [*state name and address of appointee.*]

I hereby authorize you to administer an oath [*or* oaths *as the case may be*] to [*state name of person or persons to whom, and proceeding in which the oath is to be administered or as the case may be*]

(Signed) *A.B.*, Judge,

(*or C.D.*, Surrogate Judge.)

No. 24.

FORM OF JURAT. **Section 107.**

(*Where Deponent is sworn by Interpretation.*)

On the day 18 , the said *A. B.*, was duly sworn to the truth of this affidavit by the interpretation of *C.D.*, who was previously sworn that he was well acquainted with the English and languages, and that he would faithfully interpret the said affidavit, at

Before me,

E. F., &c.

(Signed) *A.B.*

No. 25.

Section 111. **Order for Examination of Witnesses.**

In the Maritime Court of Ontario.

[*Title of Action.*]

On the day of 18 .
Before judge [*or A.B.*, surrogate judge.]

It is ordered that [*state the names of the witnesses so far as it can be done*] witnesses for the Plaintiff [*or* Defendant], shall be examined before the judge [*or* surrogate judge *or* registrar *or* deputy registrar, *or* special examiner *as the case may be*] at, [*state place of examination*], on [*state day of week*], the day of instant, [*or as the case may be*] at, o'clock in the noon.

Signed, *E.F.*
(Registrar *or* deputy registrar.)

No. 26.

Section 113. **Commission to Examine Witnesses.**

In the Maritime Court of Ontario.

(L.S.) [*Title of Action.*]

Victoria, &c.

To [*state name and address of commissioner*] Greeting.

Whereas the judge [*or* A. B., surrogate judge] of our Maritime Court of Ontario has decreed that a commission shall be issued for the examination of witnesses in the above-named action. We, therefore, hereby authorize you, upon the day of 18 , at , in the presence of the parties, their counsel, and solicitors, or in the absence of any of them, to swear the witnesses who shall be produced before you for examination in the said action, and cause them to be examined, and their evidence to be reduced into writing. We further authorize you to adjourn, if necessary, the said examination from time to time, and from place to place, as you may find expedient. And we command you, upon the examination being completed, to transmit the evidence duly certified, together with this commission, to the registry of our said court at

Given at in our said court, under the seal thereof, this day of 18 .

(Signed) *E.F.*,
Registrar, (*or* Deputy Registrar.)

Commission to examine witnesses:
Taken out by

No. 27.

Section 116. **Return to Commission to Examine Witnesses.**

In the Maritime Court of Ontario.

[*Title of Action.*]

I, *A.B.*, the commissioner named in the commission hereto annexed, bearing date the day of 18 , hereby certify as follows:

(1.) On the day of 18 , I opened the

said commission at , and in the presence of [*state who were present, whether both parties, their counsel, or solicitors, or as the case may be*], administered an oath to, and caused to be examined the under-named witnesses who were produced before me on behalf of the [*state whether Plaintiff or Defendant*] to give evidence in the above-named action; viz.:

[*Here state names of witnesses.*]

(2.) On the day of 18 , I proceeded with the examinations at the same place [*or, at some other place, as the case may be,*] and in the presence of [*state who were present, as above,*] administered an oath to and caused to be examined the under-named witnesses who were produced before me on behalf of [*state whether Plaintiff or Defendant*] to give evidence in the said action, viz.:

[*State names of witnesses.*]

(3.) Annexed hereto is the evidence of all the said witnesses certified by me to be correct.

Dated the day of 18 .

(Signed) *G.H.*,
Commissioner.

No. 28.

SHORTHAND WRITER'S OATH. Section 121.

You swear that you will faithfully report the evidence of the witnesses to be produced in this action.

So help you God.

No. 29.

NOTICE FOR HEARING. Section 132.

In the Maritime Court ot Ontario.

[*Title of Action.*]

Take notice that I set down this action for hearing

Dated the day of 18 .

(Signed) *A.B.*, Plaintiff
(*or C.D.*, Defendant.)

No. 30.

REGISTRAR'S OR DEPUTY REGISTRAR'S REPORT. Section 148.

In the Maritime Court of Ontario.

[*Title of Action.*]

To the Honorable the Judge [*or* His Honor A. B. Surrogate Judge] of the Maritime Court of Ontario.

Whereas by your decree of the 18 , you were pleased to pronounce in favor of the plaintiff [*or* Defendant], and to condemn the Defendant [*or* Plaintiff] and the ship [*or as the case may be*] in the amount to be found due to the Plaintiff [*or Defendant*] [and in costs], and you were further pleased to order that an account should be taken, and to refer the same to the registrar (*or* to the deputy registrar) [assisted by merchants] to report the amount due:

Now, I do report that I have [with the assistance of [*here state names and description of assessors, if any,*] carefully examined the accounts and vouchers and the proofs brought in by the Plaintiff [*or* Defendant] in support of his claim [*or* counterclaim], and having on the day of heard the evidence of [*state names*] who were examined as witnesses on behalf of the Defendant, [and having heard the solicitors (*or* counsel) on both sides, *or as the case may be*], I find that there is due to the Plaintiff [*or* Defendant] the sum of $ [*state sum in letters and figures*] together with interest thereon as stated in the schedule thereto annexed. I am also of opinion that the Plaintiff [*or* Defendant] is entitled to the costs of this reference [*or as the case may be*].

Dated 18 .

E. F.,
Registrar,
(*or* Deputy Registrar.)

Section 148.

SCHEDULE annexed to the forgoing report.

No.		Claimed. $	cts.	Allowed. $	cts.
1	[*Here state as briefly as possible the several items of the claim with the amount claimed and allowed on each item in the columns for figures opposite the item.*]				
2					
3					
4					
5					
&c.					
	Total				

With interest thereon from the day of 18 , at the rate of per cent, per annum, until paid.

(Signed) *E. F.*,
Registrar,
(*or* Deputy Registrar.)

No. 31.

Section 175.

COMMISSION OF APPRAISEMENT.

In the Maritime Court of Ontario.

(L.S.) *Title of Action.*

VICTORIA, &c.

To the marshal [*or A.B.*, deputy marshal] of our Maritime Court of Ontario, Greeting.

Whereas the judge [*or C.D.*, surrogate judge] of our said court has ordered that [*state whether ship or cargo, and state name of the ship and, if part only of cargo, state what part*] shall be appraised.

We, therefore, hereby command you to reduce into writing an inventory of the said [ship *or* cargo *&c.*, *as the case may be*], and having chosen one or more experienced person or persons, to swear him or them to appraise the same according to the true value thereof, and upon a certificate of such value having been reduced into writing, and signed by yourself and by the appraiser or appraisers, to file the same in the registry of our said court, together with this commission.

Given at , in our said court, under the seal thereof, this day of 18 .

(Signed) *E. F.*,
Registrar,
(*or* Deputy Registrar.)

Commission of Appraisement:
Taken out by

No. 32.

COMMISSION OF SALE. Section 175.

In the Maritime Court of Ontario.

(L.S.) [*Title of Action.*]

VICTORIA, ETC.

To the marshal *or* *A.B.*, deputy marshal] of our Maritime Court of Ontario,—Greeting.

Whereas the judge [*or* *C. D.*, surrogate judge] of our said court, has ordered that [*state whether ship or cargo and state name of ship, and if part only of cargo, what part*] shall be sold. We, therefore, hereby command you to reduce into writing an inventory of the said [ship *or* cargo, etc., *as the case may be*], and to cause the said [ship *or* cargo, etc.], to be sold by public auction for the highest price that can be obtained for the same.

And we further command you, as soon as the sale has been completed, to pay the proceeds arising therefrom into our said court, and to file an account sale signed by you, together with this commission.

Given at , in our said court, under the seal thereof, this day of 18 ,

(Signed) *E.F.*,
Registrar,
(*or* Deputy Registrar.)

Commission of sale:
Taken out by

No. 33.

COMMISSION OF APPRAISEMENT AND SALE. Section 175.

In the Maritime Court of Ontario.

(L.S.) [*Title of Action.*]

VICTORIA, ETC.

To the marshal [*or* *A.B.* deputy marshal] of our Maritime Court of Ontario.—Greeting.

Whereas the judge [*or* *C.D.* surrogate judge] of our said court, has ordered that [*state whether ship or cargo, and state name of ship, and if part only of cargo, what part*] shall be appraised and sold. We, therefore, hereby command you to reduce into writing an inventory of the said [ship or cargo, etc., *as the case may be*], and having chosen one or more experienced person or persons to swear him or them to appraise the same according to the true value thereof, and when a certificate of such value has been reduced into writing and signed by yourself and by the appraiser or appraisers, to cause the said [ship *or* cargo, etc., *as the case may be*] to be sold by public auction for the highest price, not under the appraised value thereof, that can be obtained for the same.

And we further command you, as soon as the sale has been completed, to pay the proceeds arising therefrom into our said court, and to file the said certificate of appraisement and an account sale signed by you, together with this commission.

Given at , in our said court, under the seal thereof, this day of 18 .

(Signed) *E.F.*,
Registrar,
(*or* Deputy Registrar.)

Commission of appraisement and sale :
Taken out by

No. 34.

Section 175.

COMMISSION OF REMOVAL.

In the Maritime Court of Ontario.

(L.S.) [*Title of Action.*]

VICTORIA, ETC.

To the marshal [*or A.B.* deputy marshal] of our Maritime Court of Ontario,—Greeting.

Whereas the judge, [*or C.D.* surrogate judge] of our said court, has ordered that the [*state name and description of ship*] shall be removed from to on a policy of insurance in the sum of $ being deposited in the registry of our said court ; and whereas a policy of insurance for the said sum has been so deposited. We, therefore, hereby command you to cause the said ship to be removed accordingly. And we further command you, as soon as the removal has been completed, to file a certificate thereof, signed by you, in the said registry, together with this commission.

Given at , in our said court, under the seal thereof, this day of 18 .

(Signed) *E.F.*
Registrar,
(*or* Deputy Registrar.)

Commission of removal :
Taken out by .

No. 35.

Section 175.

COMMISSION FOR DISCHARGE OF CARGO.

In the Maritime Court of Ontario.

(L.S.) [*Title of Action.*]

VICTORIA, &c.

To the marshal [*or A. B.* deputy marshal] of our Maritime Court of Ontario,—Greeting.

Whereas the judge [*or C. D.* surrogate judge] of our said court, has ordered that the cargo of the ship shall be discharged. We therefore hereby command you to discharge the said cargo from on board the said ship, and to put the same into some fit and proper place of deposit. And we further command you, as soon as the discharge of the said cargo has been completed, to file your certificate thereof in the registry of our said court, together with this commission.

Given at in our said court, under the seal thereof, this day of 18 .

(Signed) *E. F.*,
Registrar,
(*or* Deputy Registrar.)

Commission for discharge of cargo :
Taken out by .

No. 36.

BILL OF SALE.

Section 178.

OFFICIAL NUMBER OF SHIP................ NAME OF SHIP................

Port Number and Year of Registry.	Port of Registry	British or Foreign built..	How propelled....	Where built....	When built....

			Feet.	Tenths.
Number of Deck ...... Number of Masts...... Rigged................ Stern	Build................. Galleries .... Head................. Framework	Length from forepart of Stem, under the bowsprit, to the aft side of the Head of the Stern-post .... Main breadth to outside of Plank .... Depth in Hold from Tonnage Deck to Ceiling at Midships.... Depth in Hold from Upper Deck to Ceiling at Midships in the case of three Decks and upwards.................. Length of Engine Room, if any...		

PARTICULARS OF ENGINES (IF ANY)	No. of Engines.	Description.	Whether British or Foreign made.	When made.	Name and Address of Makers.	Diameter of Cylinders.	Length of Stroke.	No. of Horse-Power combined.

GROSS TONNAGE.	No. of Tons.	DEDUCTIONS ALLOWED.	No. of Tons.
Under Tonnage Deck .... Closed-in Spaces above Tonnage Deck, if any, Space or Spaces between Decks .... Poop .... Forecastle .... Roundhouse .... Other Closed-in Spaces, if any, as follows		On account of Space required for Propelling Power .... On account of Spaces occupied by Seamen or Apprentices, appropriated to their use and kept free from Goods and Stores of every kind not being the personal property of the Crew. These spaces are the following, viz.:	
Gross Tonnage .... Deductions as per Contra		Total Deductions	
Registered Tonnage..........................			

I,............of the..........of..........in the County of..........and Province of Ontario, Marshal*, of the Maritime Court of Ontario, in consideration of the sum of..............paid to me by................, the Receipt whereof is hereby acknowledged, transfer..............Shares in the Ship above particularly described, and in her boats, guns, ammunition, small arms, and appurtenances, to the said....... ....who has purchased the same at a sale held by me as such Marshal*, under and in pursuance of a commission of appraisement and sale, (or "commission of sale," or "order for sale," or as the case may be) to me directed by the said Court, in a certain action therein pending at............, numbered†......, styled‡........bearing date the...........day of............, A.D. 188 §

In witness whereof I have hereunto subscribed my name and affixed the seal of said Court, this........day of.........., one thousand eignt hundred and eighty-....

Executed by the above-named................in the presence of................

* Or "Deputy Marshal." † Number of action. ‡ Style of action in which sale was held. § Date of commission or order for sale.

Section 182.

No. 37.

ORDER FOR INSPECTION.

In the Maritime Court of Ontario.

[*Title of Action.*]

On the day of 18 .
Before

Judge [*or A.B.* Surrogate Judge].

The judge [*or* surrogate judge] on the application of [*state whether Plaintiff or Defendant*] ordered that the ship should be inspected by [*state whether by the marshal or by the assessors of the court, or, as the case may be,*] and that a report in writing of the inspection should be lodged by him [or them] in the registry.

(Signed) *E.F.*,
Registrar.
(*or* Deputy Registrar.)

No. 38.

Section 185.

NOTICE OF DISCONTINUANCE.

In the Maritime Court of Ontario.

[*Title of Action.*]

Take notice that this action is discontinued.

Dated the day of 18 .

(Signed) *A.B.*, Plaintiff.

No. 39.

Section 185.

NOTICE TO ENTER JUDGMENT FOR COSTS.

In the Maritime Court of Ontario.

[*Title of Action.*]

Take notice that I apply to have judgment entered for my costs in this action.

Dated the day of 18 .

(Signed) *C.D.*, Defendant.

No. 40.

Section 187.

NOTICE OF APPEAL.

In the Maritime Court of Ontario.

[*Title of Action.*]

Take notice that I, *A.B.*, Plaintiff [*or* Defendant] appeal from the decree [*or* order] of the judge [*or A.B.*, surrogate judge] of the said court made the day of 18 , to the Supreme Court of Canada.

Dated the day of 18 .

(Signed) *A.B.*, Plaintiff.
or Defendant.

No. 41.

Section 202.

NOTICE FOR CAVEAT WARRANT.

In the Maritime Court of Ontario.

Take notice that I, *A.B.* of apply for a caveat against the issue of any warrant for the arrest of [*state name and nature of property*], and

I undertake within *three days* after being required to do so, to give bail to any action or counterclaim that may have been or may be brought against the same in this court in a sum not exceeding [*state sum in letters*] dollars, or to pay such sum into court.

My address for service is

Dated the day of 18 .

(Signed) *A.B.*

No. 42.

CAVEAT WARRANT. Section 202.

In the Maritime Court of Ontario.

[*State Name of Ship, &c.*]

Caveat entered this day of 18 , against the issue of any warrant for the arrest of [*state name and nature of property*], without notice being first given to [*state name and address of person to whom, and address at which notice is to be given*], who has undertaken to give bail to any action or counterclaim that may have been or may be brought in the said court against the said [*state name and nature of property*].

On withdrawal of caveat add—

Caveat withdrawn the day of 18 .

No. 43.

NOTICE FOR CAVEAT RELEASE. Section 203.

In the Maritime Court of Ontario.

[*Title of Action.*]

Take notice that I, *A.B.*, Plaintiff [*or* Defendant] in the above named action, apply for a caveat against the release of [*state name and nature of property*].

[*If the person applying for the caveat is not a party to the action, he must also state his address and an address for service within three miles of the registry.*]

Dated the day of 18 ,

(Signed) *A.B*

No. 44.

CAVEAT RELEASE. Section 203.

In the Maritime Court of Ontario.

[*Title of Action.*]

Caveat entered this day of 18 , against the issue of any release of [*state name and address of person entering caveat, and his address for service*].

On withdrawal of caveat, add—

Caveat withdrawn this day of , 18 .

No. 45.

NOTICE FOR CAVEAT PAYMENT. Section 204.

In the Maritime Court of Ontario.

[*Title of Action.*]

Take notice that *I, A.B.*, Plaintiff [*or* Defendant] in the above-named action, apply for a caveat against the payment of any money [*if for costs, add* for costs, *or as the case may be*] out of the proceeds of the sale of [*state whether ship or cargo, and name of ship, &c.*], now remaining in court, without notice being first given to me.

[*If the person applying for the caveat is not a party to the action, he must also state his address, and an address for service within three miles of the registry.*]

Dated the day of 18 .

(Signed) *A.B.*

No. 46.

Section 204.

CAVEAT PAYMENT.

In the Maritime Court of Ontario.

[*Title of Action.*]

Caveat entered this day of 18 , against the payment of any money [*if for costs, add* for costs, *or as the case may be*] out of the proceeds of the sale of [*state whether ship or cargo; and if ship, state name of ship, &c*] now remaining in court, without notice being first given to [*state name and address of person to whom, and address at which notice is to be given*].

On withdrawal of the caveat, add—

Caveat withdrawn this day of , 18 .

No. 47.

Section 210.

NOTICE FOR WITHDRAWAL OF CAVEAT.

In the Maritime Court of Ontario.

[*Title of Action.*]

Take notice that I withdraw the caveat [*state whether caveat warrant, release or payment*] entered by me in this action [*or as the case may be*].

Dated the day of , 18 .

(Signed) *A.B.*

No. 48.

Section 213.

SUBPŒNA.

In the Maritime Court of Ontario.

(L.S.) [*Title of Action.*]

VICTORIA, &c.

To Greeting.

We commend you that, all other things set aside, you appear in person before the judge [*or* surrogate judge, *or* the registrar, *or* deputy registrar, *or G.H.*, a commissioner appointed by an order of our said Court *or* A.B., an examiner] at on the day of 18 , at o'clock in the noon of the same day, and so from day to day as may be required, and give evidence in the above-named action.

And herein fail not at your peril.

Given at , in our said court, under the seal thereof, this day of , 18 .

Subpœna:

Taken out by

No. 49.

Subpœna Duces Tecum. Section 213.

The same as the preceding form, adding before the words, "And "herein fail not at your peril," *the words,* "and that you bring with you "for production before the said judge [*or* surrogate judge, registrar *or* "deputy registrar *or* commissioner, *or* examiner, *as the case may be*] the "following documents, viz.

[*Here state the documents required to be produced.*]

No. 50.

Order for Payment. Section 216.

In the Maritime Court of Ontario.

(L.S.) [*Title of Action.*]

On the day of 18

Before judge [*or* Surrogate judge.]

It is ordered that *A.B.*, [Plaintiff *or* Defendant, etc.,] do pay to *C.D.* [Defendant *or* Plaintiff, etc.] within days from the date hereof the sum of $ [*state sum in letters and figures*] being the amount [*or* balance of the amount] found due from the said *A.B.* to the said *C.D.* for [*state whether for damages, salvage, or costs, or as the case may be*] in the above-named action.

(Signed) *E.F.*,
Registrar,
(*or* Deputy Registrar.)

No. 51.

Attachment. Section 217.

In the Maritime Court of Ontario.

(L.S.)

Victoria, by the Grace of God of the United Kingdom of Great Britain and Ireland, Queen, Defender of the Faith.

To all and singular our justices of the peace, sheriffs, bailiffs, marshals, deputy marshals, constables, and to all our officers, ministers, and others whomsoever:—Greeting.

Whereas in a cause of instituted in the Maritime Court of Ontario on behalf of against [and against intervening], the said court has decreed [*name*] to be attached for [his] manifest contumacy and contempt in [*set out contempt shortly*].

We, therefore, hereby command you to attach and arrest the said and to keep [him] under safe and secure arrest and bring him before our judge [*or A.B.*, our surrogate judge].

Given under the seal of our said court at this day of

Attachment: By the Court.

Taken out by (Signed) *E.F.*,
Registrar,
(*or* Deputy Registrar,)
at .

No. 52.

Section 218.

ORDER FOR COMMITTAL.

In the Maritime Court of Ontario.

(L.S.) [*Title of Action.*]

On the day of 18 .
Before Judge [*or A.B.* Surrogate Judge].

Whereas *C.D.* [*state name and description of person to be committed*] has committed a contempt of court in that [*state in what the contempt consists*] and, having been this day brought before the judge [*or A.B.* surrogate judge] on attachment, persists in his said contempt, it is now ordered that he be committed to prison for the term of from the date the date hereof, or until he shall clear himself from his said contempt

(Signed) *E.F.*,
Registrar (*or* Deputy Registrar).

No. 53.

Section 218.

COMMITTAL.

To the Keepers of the common goals.

In the Maritime Court of Ontario.

Receive into your custody the body [*or* bodies] of herewith sent to you, for the cause herein-under written; that is to say,—

For [*State briefly the ground of attachment*].

Dated the day of 18 .

(Signed) *J.K.*,
Judge (*or* Surrogate Judge).

Witness,
E.F.,
Registrar (*or* Deputy Registrar.)

No. 54.

WRIT OF EXECUTION (FIERI FACIAS, GOODS OR LANDS.) Section 220.

In the Maritime Court of Ontario.

(L.S.) [*Title of Action.*]

Issued from the office of the Registrar or Deputy Registrar of the Maritime Court of Ontario, at , in the County of
Registrar [or Deputy Registrar].

VICTORIA, by the Grace of God of the United Kingdom of Great Britain and Ireland, Queen, Defender of the Faith.

To the marshal and each deputy marshal of the Maritime Court of Ontario,— GREETING:

Whereas on the day of , 18 , obtained a decree [*or* order] of this court against for the sum of and costs, and it was thereupon ordered by the court that should pay the same to [on the day of *or* forthwith, *as the case may be*].

And whereas default has been in payment according to the said decree [*or* order].

We therefore hereby command you, that you cause to be made of the goods and chattels of the said wheresoever they may be found within the Province of Ontario, the sum of being the amount due to under the said decree [*or* order] including the costs of this writ and incidental thereto, or such part or so much thereof as may be sufficient to satisfy this writ and the costs of executing the same, together with interest at the rate of six per centum per annum on the said sum from the day of and to pay what you have so made to the [*here designate the proper person entitled thereto, as the case may be*] and make return of what you have done under this writ, immediately upon the execution thereof, and have there then this writ.

Given under the seal of our said Court at this day of 18 .

By the Court.
(Signed) A. B., Registrar (*or* Deputy Registrar.)

(*a*) If writ be for non-payment of costs, or moneys ordered to be paid under a special order, as the case may be, the above form may be varied accordingly.

(*b*) If writ be against lands, the words "goods and chattels" may be omitted and the words "lands and tenements" inserted.

No. 55.

MINUTE OF FILING ANY DOCUMENT. Section 226.

In the Maritime Court of Ontario.

[*Title of Action.*]

I, *A. B.*, [*state whether Plaintiff or Defendant*], file the following documents, viz.:

[*Here describe the documents filed.*]

Dated the day of 18

(Signed) *A. B.*

No. 56.

Section 239. **FORM OF SECURITY, BY MARSHAL OR DEPUTY MARSHAL.**

Know all men by these presents that we, *A.B.*, marshal [*or* deputy marshal] of the Maritime Court of Ontario; *C. D.*, of in the county of , and *E. F.*, of in the county of , do hereby jointly and severally for ourselves and each of our heirs, executors and administrators, covenant and promise that the said *A. B.*, as marshal [*or* deputy marshal] of the Maritime Court of Ontario shall well and truly pay over to the court all such moneys as he shall receive by virtue of his said office of marshal [*or* deputy marshal].

And that he shall not willfully misconduct himself in his said office to the damage of any person being a party in any proceeding in the said court.

Nevertheless it is hereby declared that no greater sum shall be recovered under this covenant against the said parties hereto than as follows, that is to say:—Against the said *A. B.* in the whole dollars. Against the said *C. D.*, in the whole dollars. Against the said *E. F.*. in the whole. dollars.

In witness whereof we have to these presents set our hands and seals this day of , 18 .

Signed, sealed and delivered, in the presence of

No. 57.

Section 239. **AFFIDAVIT OF JUSTIFICATION.**

In the Maritime Court of Ontario.

County of

I, *A. B.*, the principal covenantor in the annexed covenant named (*or* one of the sureties in the annexed covenant named) do make oath and say as follows:—

1. That I am seized and possessed to my own use of real estate in Ontario to the actual value of dollars over and above all charges upon or encumbrances affecting the same.
2. The said real estate consists of (describe property.)
3. I am worth dollars (the amount of which the parties become liable by the covenant) over and above my just debts.
4. My post office address is as follows:—

(Signed) A. B.

Sworn before me at
in the county of
the day of 18 .

A Commissioner, &c.

No. 58.

Section 249. **MINUTE OF ORDER OF COURT.**

In the Maritime Court of Ontario.

[*Title of Action.*]

On the day of 18 .
Before
Judge [*or A.B.* Surrogate Judge.]

The judge [*or A.B.* surrogate judge], on the application of [*state whether Plaintiff or Defendant*] ordered [*state purport of order*].

No. 59.

MINUTE ON EXAMINATION OF WITNESSES. **Section 249.**

In the Maritime Court of Ontario.

[*Title of Action.*]

On the day of 18 .
Before
Judge [*or* Surrogate Judge].

A.B. [*state whether Plaintiff or Defendant*] produced as witnesses.

[*Here state names of witnesses in full.*]

who, having been sworn [*or as the case may be*], were examined orally [*if by interpretation, add* by interpretation of .]

No. 60.

MINUTE OF DECREE. **Section 249.**

In the Maritime Court of Ontario.

[*Title of Action.*]

On the day of 18 .
Before ,
Judge [*or* Surrogate Judge.]

(1) *Decree for an ascertained sum:*

The judge [*or A.B.*, surrogate judge] having heard [*state whether Plaintiff and Defendant, or their counsel or solicitors, or as the case may be*], and having been assisted by [*state names and descriptions of assessors, if any*] pronounced the sum of [*state sum in letters and figures*] to be due to the Plaintiff [*or* Defendant], in respct of his claim [*or* counterclaim], together with costs [*if the decree is for costs.*] And he condemned—

(a.) *in an Action in rem where Bail has not been given;*
the ship [*or* cargo *ex* the ship , *or* proceeds of the ship , *or* of the cargo *ex* the ship *or as the case may be*] in the said sum [and in costs].

(b.) *in an Action in personam, or in rem where Bail has been given;*
the Defendant [*or* Plaintiff] and his bail [*if bail has been given*] in the said sum [and in costs].

(2.) *Decree for a sum not ascertained:*

The judge [*or* surrogate judge] having heard, &c. [*as above*] pronounced in favour of the Plaintiff's claim [*or* Defendant's counterclaim] and condemned the ship (*or* cargo, *&c.*.) *or* the Defendant [*or* Plaintiff] and his bail [*if bail has been given*] in the amount to be found due to the Plaintiff [*or* Defendant] [and in costs]. And he ordered that an account should be taken, and

(a.) *if the amount is to be assessed by the judge* [*or surrogate judge*],
that all accounts and vouchers, with the proofs in support thereof, should be filed within *days* [*or as the case may be.*]

(b.) *if the judge or surrogate judge refers the assessment to the registrar or deputy registrar,*
referred the same to the registrar (*or* deputy registrar) [assisted by merchants], to report the amount due, and ordered that all accounts, &c. *as* [*above*].

(3.) Decree on dismissal of action:

The judge [*or surrogate judge*] having heard, &c. [*as above*] dismissed the action [*if with costs add*] and condemned the plaintiff and his bail [*if bail has been given*] in costs.

No. 61.

Section 249.

MINUTES IN AN ACTION FOR DAMAGE BY COLLISION.

A.B., &c.

No

against

The Ship "Mary."

18	
Jan. 3	A writ of summons [and a warrant] was [*or* were] issued to X.Y., on behalf of A.B., &c., the owners of the ship "Jane" against the ship "Mary" [and freight, *or as the case may be*] in an action for damage by collision. Amount claimed $5,000.
" 5	Y.Z. filed notice of appearance on behalf of C.D., &c., the owners of the ship "Mary."
" 6	X.Y., filed writ of summons.
" "	The marshal [*or* deputy marshal] filed warrant.
" 7	Y.Z., filed bailbond to answer judgment as against the Defendants [*or as the case may be*] in the sum of $5,000, with affidavit of service of notice of bail.
" "	A release of the ship "Mary" was issued to Y.Z.
" 8	X.Y. filed preliminary act [and notice of motion for the pleadings].
" "	Y.Z. filed preliminary act.
" 10	The judge [*or* surrogate judge] having heard solicitors on both sides [*or as the case may be*] ordered pleadings to be filed.
" 11	X.Y. filed petition.
" 14	Y.Z. filed answer [and counterclaim].
" 15	X.Y. filed reply.
" 16	The judge [*or* surrogate judge] having heard solicitors on both sides [*or as the case may be*] ordered both Plaintiffs and Defendants to file affidavits of discovery, and to produce, if required, for mutual inspection, the documents therein set forth within *three days*.
" 18	X. Y. filed affidavit of discovery.
" 19	Y. Z. filed affidavit of discovery.
" 22	X. Y. filed notice of trial.
" 26	X. Y. produced as witnesses [*state names of witnesses*], who, having been sworn, were examined orally in court, the said [*state names*] having been sworn and examined by interpretation of [*state name of interpreter*] interpreter of the language. Present [*state names of assessors present, if any*] assessors.
	Y. Z. produced as witnesses, &c., [*as above*]
	The judge [*or* surrogate judge] having heard [*state whether Plaintiffs and Defendants, or their counsel or solicitors, as the case may be*], and having been assisted by [*state names and descriptions of assessors, if any*], pronounced in favor of the Plaintiffs [*or* Defendants] and condemned the Defendants [*or* Plaintiffs] and their bail [*if bail has been given*]

18	in the amounts to be found due to the Plaintiffs [*or* Defendants] [and in costs]. And he ordered that an account should be taken, and referred the same to the registrar [assisted by merchants] to report the amount due, and ordered that all accounts and vouchers, with proofs in support thereof, should be filed within *days* [*or as the case may be*].
Feb. 5	X.Y. filed statement of claim, with accounts and vouchers in support thereof [numbered 1 to], and affidavits of [*state names of deponents, if any*].
" 8	Y.Z. filed accounts and vouchers [numbered 1 to] in answer to claim.
" 9	X.Y. filed notice for hearing of reference.
" 15	X.Y. [*or* Y. Z.] filed registrar's [*or* deputy registrar's] report, &c.

Here insert address for service of documents required to be served on the Plaintiffs.	*Here insert address for service of documents rebuired to be served on the Defendants.*

Note.—The above minutes are given as such as might ordinarily be required in an action *in rem* for damage by collision, where pleadings have been ordered. In some actions many of these minutes would be superfluous. In others additional minutes would be required.

SCHEDULE B.

Section 254. TABLES OF FEES TO BE TAKEN BY SOLICITORS, COUNSEL, REGISTRAR AND DEPUTY REGISTRARS, SPECIAL OR OTHER EXAMINERS, OFFICIAL REPORTER, MARSHAL AND DEPUTY MARSHALS, APPRAISERS, WITNESSES, AND GOVERNMENT FEE FUND.

I.—BY THE SOLICITOR.

1. *Instructions.*

1.	Instructions for suit or to defend	$ 3 00
2.	Instructions for suit or to defend when no warrant is issued	2 00
3.	Instructions to counsel in special matters	1 00
4.	Instructions to counsel in common matters	0 50
5.	Instructions for special affidavit when allowed by taxing officer	1 00
6.	Instructions for statement of claim or defence or counterclaim	1 50
7.	Instructions to amend any pleading when amendment is proper	2 00
8.	Instructions for special case in course of action to add parties by order of judge or surrogate	2 00
9.	Instructions for brief	2 00
10.	Instructions for adding parties in consequence of marriage, death, assignment, &c.	1 00
11.	Instructions to defend added parties	2 00
12.	Instructions for such other important step or proceeding in the action as the taxing officer is satisfied warrants such a charge	2 00

2. *Writs.*

13.	All writs (except writs of execution and concurrent writs)	1 00
14.	Concurrent writ	0 75
15.	Renewed writ (except writ of execution)	1 00
16.	On all writs for every folio over 4	0 20
17.	Notice of writ under Sec. 16 (including copy)	1 00
18.	Special indorsement on writ of summons	0 50
19.	Writ of execution	4 00
	Renewal of writ of execution	3 00
	(In both cases to include placing the same in the marshal's or deputy marshal's hands, and all attendances, indorsements and letters in connection therewith.)	

3. *Copy and Service of Writs.*

20.	For copy including copy of notices required to be indorsed	0 50
21.	If over 4 folios, for each additional folio	0 10
22.	Service of each copy (if not done by marshal or deputy marshal or substitute)	1 00
23.	Mileage, if over 2 miles, for each additional mile	0 13
24.	For service of writ out of jurisdiction, such allowance as judge or surrogate shall think fit.	

4. *Drawing Pleadings, &c.*

25.	Statement of claim or defence or statement of defence and counterclaim not exceeding 10 folios (including copy to keep)	2 00
26.	For every additional folio	0 20
27,	Other pleadings per folio	0 20
28.	Special case per folio	0 20
29.	Interrogatories, &c., per folio	0 20
	(The above charges do not include engrossing, or copies to file or serve.)	
30.	In collision cases preliminary acts not exceeding 10 folios	2 00
	For every additional folio	0 20

5. *Copies of Pleadings, &c.*

No.	Item	Fee
31.	Pleadings, brief and other documents when no other provision is made; for copies properly allowable, per folio	0 10
32.	Certified copies of pleadings, &c., for use of judge or surrogate	2 00
33.	For every folio over 20	0 10
34.	Copies of orders or other documents for service or for filing, per folio.	0 10
35.	Observations and other original matter in brief, per folio	0 20
36.	Notices, including one copy of appearance when duly entered and notice given on day of appearance, but not otherwise	0 50
37.	To consul or officer under Sec. 36	0 50
38.	If over 3 folios, each additional folio	0 20
39.	Notice to admit and produce, not over 2 folios and one copy	0 50
40.	For each additional folio	0 20
41.	Other notices (common)	0 50
42.	Notice of setting down	0 50
43.	Notice of motion in court or chambers and copy to serve, per folio, including engrossing	0 30
44.	Each necessary additional copy of any of above notices for service, per folio	0 10
45.	Notice of discontinuance and one copy	0 50

6. *Perusals.*

No.	Item	Fee
46.	Of statement of claim, defence, defence and counterclaim	1 00
47.	Of special case, except the one by whom prepared, when case is submitted in course of cause	2 00
48.	Interrogatories and cross-interrogatories or interrogatories on commission	1 00
	(To be increased in discretion of taxing officer to $5.00.	
49.	Of affidavits of party adverse in interest filed or produced on any application, when perusal necessary, 20 folios or under	1 00
	Every folio over 20, per folio	0 05
	(Not to exceed in any case $5 00.)	

7. *Attendances.*

No.	Item	Fee
50.	Necessary attendances consequent upon service of notice to produce or to admit, or inspection of documents under order, including making admission	1 00
	To be increased by taxing officer in a case of special, difficult or important nature to	2 00
51.	In chambers, on return of motion	1 00
	To be increased in discretion of judge or surrogate to a sum not exceeding	5 00
52.	On counsel, consultation in special, important or difficult matter	2 00
	To be increased by judge or surrogate to a sum not exceeding	5 00
	(No special attendance to be allowed to solicitor on proceeding when he also acts as counsel.)	
53.	Solicitor attending court on trial of action, when not himself counsel or partner of the counsel	2 00
	In special, important or difficult cases, each hour necessarily present at trial	1 50
	Not to exceed per day	10 00
	(Provided such attendance of solicitor and length of time be noted at the time in book of officer of court present at the time or be proved by affidavit.)	
54.	To hear judgment, when not given at close of argument or when judgment reserved, each attendance	2 00
55.	On taxation of costs, per hour	1 00
56.	On revision of costs, per hour	1 00
57.	To obtain or give undertaking to appear, when service accepted by solicitor	1 00
58.	Attendance to file or serve	0 50
59.	Attendance on appointment of registrar, deputy registrar, or examiner, per hour	1 00
	To be increased in discretion of surrogate or registrar to	2 00
60.	Every other necessary attendance	0 50
61.	On important points and matters requiring attendance of counsel the registrar, deputy registrar or examiner may certify amount of counsel fee proper to be allowed (to be noted at the time) for guidance of judge or surrogate who may allow same in lieu of fees for attendance.	

8. *Affidavits.*

62. Drawing affidavits, per folio 0
63. Common affidavits of service to include attendance to swear, and oath, 1
64. Engrossing affidavits to have sworn, per folio 0
65. Copies of affidavits when necessary, per folio 0 20
66. The solicitor for preparing each exhibit .... 0 [illegible]

9. *Briefs.*

67. For drawing briefs, 5 folios or under 2 00
68. For each folio above 5 .... 0 10
69. For drawing brief, per folio, for original and necessary matter 0 20
70. Copy of documents other than pleadings, per folio 0 10
71. Copy of brief for second counsel, when fee taxed to him, per folio 0 10
72. { Appearance by defendant, including attending to enter same 1 00
If over five folios, per folio 0 20
For every additional defendant .... 0 20 }

10. *Judgments, or Orders.*

73. Drawing minutes of judgment or order, per folio, when prepared by solicitor under directions of judge or surrogate, or registrar or deputy registrar 0 20
74. Judgment for non-appearance on specially indorsed writs 1 00
75. Attending for appointment to settle or pass judgment, or order of court, copy and service 1 00
76. When served on more than one party, the extra copies and services are to be allowed.
77. { For every hour's attendance before proper officer on settling or passing minutes 1 00
To be increased in the discretion of the taxing officer in special and difficult cases, when the solicitor attends personally, to a sum not exceeding altogether .... 5 00 }

11. *Letters.*

78. Letter to each defendant before suit, only one letter to be allowed to any defendants who are in partnership and when subject of suit relates to the transaction of their partnership 0 50
79. Common letters, including necessary agency letters 0 50
80. With power to the registrar or deputy registrar as between solicitor and client, to increase the fee for special and important letters, to an amount not exceeding 2 00
81. Postages—the amount actually disbursed.

12. *Statements.*

82. Statements of issues in registrar's or deputy registrar's office when required by them 2 00
83. For each folio over 10 .... 0 20

II.—Counsel Fees.

84. On argument in chambers in cases proper for the attendance of counsel (to be increased in the discretion of the judge or surrogate to a sum not exceeding $10.00 to be marked at the time) 2 00
85. Fee on settling pleadings, replications (when special) and advising whether cause should be set down for examination and hearing, and advising on evidence (to be increased in the discretion of the judge or surrogate to a sum not exceeding $10.00) 2 00
86. On special applications to the court,, (to be increased in the discretion of the judge or surrogate only) 5 00
87. Fee to be allowed on settling special affidavits used in court (to be increased at the discretion of the registrar or deputy registrar to a sum not exceeding $5.00) 2 00
88. On special and important points and matters requiring the attendance of counsel, the judge or surrogate, registrar or deputy registrar or special examiner may, in lieu of the fees for attendance, allow a counsel fee when counsel attended the same, (to be noted at the time) not to exceed 5 00

89. Fee on consultation when necessary 5 00
90. Fee with brief at trial 10 00
(To be increased by judge or surrogate at his discretion.)
91. To attend reference to registrar or deputy registrar, when counsel necessary 5 00
(To be increased in special and important matters requiring the attendance of counsel by the judge or surrogate upon notice to the opposite party.)

III.—Miscellaneous.

92. When it has been satisfactorily proved that proceedings have been taken by solicitor out of court to expedite proceedings, save costs, or compromise suits, an allowance is to be made therefor in the discretion of the judge or surrogate.
93. Drawing judge's or surrogate's appointment, and attendance for his signature and to serve 1 00
(When served on more than one party the extra copies and services shall be allowed.)
94. Drawing bill of costs as between party and party for taxation, including engrossing and copy for taxing officer, per folio 0 30
95. Copy, per folio, to serve 0 10
96. The registrar or deputy registrar in taxing costs between solicitor and client or between party and party may allow for services rendered, not provided for by this tariff, a reasonable compensation as far as practicable analogous to its provisions, not in any case to exceed the fees allowed for similar services by the tariff of the Supreme Court of Judicature for Ontario, if therein provided for.

IV.—Court Fees.

97. Fee on certified copy of pleading for judge or surrogate 1 00
98. Fee on every order or judgment to the party obtaining the same 1 00

V.—Disbursements.

1. *Fees to be taken by the Registrar or Deputy Registrar.*

99. Every writ of summons 0 50
100. Entering appearance and filing memorandum thereof 0 20
101. Filing statement of claim 0 20
102. Filing statement of defence or counterclaim 0 20
103. Entering and filing all other proceedings and affidavits on production, interrogatories and other depositions or other evidence 0 20
104. Filing other papers 0 10
105. Every instrument under seal of court for which a fee is not specially named 1 00
106. Certificate of arrest 1 00
107. Amending every writ or other proceeding 0 30
108. Instructions under Sec. 45 .... 0 50
109. Every attendance on warrant or appointment, not exceeding one hour 1 00
110. Every additional hour, or less 1 00
111. Filing preliminary acts 0 50
112. Filing special case 0 50
113. Certificates of not more than 2 folios, to include forwarding same under rules, except postage 0 50
114. For each additional folio 0 20
115. Notice to assessors, each 0 25
116. Setting down for trial 4 00
117. Forwarding papers from one office to that of another 0 50
(And postage or express charges.)
118. Drawing report on reference or decree or court order when prepared by registrar or deputy registrar of not more than 3 folios 1 00
119. For each additional folio 0 20
120. Each notice from registry not otherwise provided for 0 25
121. Notice of sale, or notice of proceeding in cause of possession 0 75
122. Each direction to the bank to receive money 0 50
123. Fee on filing receipt and papers from deputy registrar on payment into court 0 25

fee for caveat,
" " making O.C.

124. Deputy registrar forwarding receipt and papers as to payment to registrar	0 25
125. Subpœna, including præcipe	0 50
126. Fee to registrar entering institution af action in book whether at head office or deputy registrar's	0 60
127. Fee to deputy registrar sending notice	0 25
128. Order in chambers, including entering	0 50
129. Entering decrees and other orders per folio	0 10
130. Copy of papers required to be given out, per folio	0 10
131. Searches within one year, each	0 10
132. Searches extending over one year and within two years	0 20
133. Searches extending over two years or a general search	0 50
134. Every affidavit, oath or affirmation taken	0 20
135. Marking each exhibit	0 20
136. Every appointment	0 50
137. Each attendance on reference or other special matter per hour, or enlargement thereof	1 00
138. Attending the opening of a commission	1 00
139. Every commission for examination of witnesses or parties	1 00
140. Each verdict taken, non suit, record withdrawn, or rule or order of reference at trial	1 00
141. Attending on inspection of documents produced with affidavit on production, per hour	1 00
142. Taxing costs, per hour	1 00

2. *Fees to be taken by the Registrar only.*

143. Countersigning cheque for payment of money out of court, if sum paid out does not exceed $500.00	0 50
144. For every additional $500.00	0 50

3. *Fees to be taken by a Special Examiner or Registrar or Deputy Registrar acting as Examiner.*

145. Every appointment	0 50
146. Every oath	0 20
147. Marking exhibit	0 20
148. Attendance per hour	1 50
149. Fair copy for solicitor, per folio (when required)	0 10
150. Every certificate	0 50
151. Making up and forwarding answers, depositions, etc	0 40
152. Every attendance out of office within two miles	2 00
153. Every such attendance, over 2 miles, every extra mile	0 20
154. Every such attendance, when either solicitor or witness does not attend, and examiner not previously notified	1 00

Section 123.

4. *Fees to be taken by Official Reporter.*

155. For every day's attendance in court	5 00
156. For first copy of evidence if required by party, or by judge or surrogate, per folio	0 10
157. Eor each additional copy, per folio	0 05

5. *Fees to be taken by the Marshal or Deputy Marshal.*

158. Receiving, filing, entering and indorsing every paper	0 25
159. Attendance to swear all necessary affidavits	0 50
160. On the execution of every warrant	2 00
161. Service of writ of summons *in personam*, each defendant	1 00
162. Serving subpœnas, rules, notices or other papers, (besides mileage)	0 50
163. Actual and necessary mileage from the court house to the place where service of any process, paper or proceeding is made, per mile	0 13
164. On the execution of attachment for every person attached	2 00
165. On the execution of every decree or commission of un-livery, appraisement or sale	2 00
166. On the execution of every other instrument for which a fee is not specially provided	1 00
167. On attending, appointing and swearing appraisers, each	1 00
168. On delivering up ship, vessel, goods or property to the purchaser agreeably to the inventory	2 00
169. Fee on bill of sale of ship	1 00

170.	On attending the un-livery of the cargo, or sale of ship, or vessel, or goods, per day	2 00
171.	On retaining possession of a ship or vessel, or of ship or vessel and goods, per day	0 50
	Exclusive of such reasonable disbursements actually incurred in the custody thereof as the registrar or deputy registrar may allow, not exceeding per day of 24 hours	2 00
	(If the marshal or deputy marshal or any of his substitutes is required to go a greater distance than five miles from his office to perform any of the above duties, he will be entitled to his reasonable expenses for travelling, board and maintenance, as the registrar or deputy registrar may allow.)	
172.	Poundage on the proceeds of any vessel, goods or property sold under the decree or order of the court if under $250.00	1 00
173.	If over $250.00 and not exceeding $500.00	2 00
174.	For every additional $500.00	0 50
175.	Calling each cause at the hearing in court	1 00
176.	Calling each witness	0 10

6. *Fees to be taken by Appraisers.*

177.	Each, per appraisement	2 50
	(To be increased to a sum not exceeding $5.00 in the discretion of the registrar or deputy registrar.)	

7. *Fees to be taken by Assessors.*

Section 130.

178.	Each, per day (to be distributed ratably among the causes if more than one tried in a day	6 00

8. *Allowance to Witnesses.*

179.	To witness residing not more than three miles from the place to which summoned, per day	1 00
180.	To witness residing over three miles from such place	1 25
181.	Barristers and attorneys and solicitors, physicians and surgeons, when called upon to give evidence in consequence of any professional service rendered by them or to give opinions, per day	4 00
182.	Engineers and surveyors, when called upon to give evidence of any professional service rendered by them, or to give evidence depending upon their skill or judgment, per day	4 00
183.	If the witnesses attend in one cause only, they will be entitled to the full allowance.	
184.	If they attend in more than one cause they will be entitled to a proportionate part in each cause only.	
185.	The travelling expenses of witnesses over ten miles, shall be allowed according to the sums reasonably and actually paid, but in no case shall exceed twenty cents per mile one way.	

9. *Government Fee Fund.*

186.	On every writ by which action is commenced	2 00
187.	On every appearance and pleading filed	1 00
188.	On every replication filed	1 00
189.	On every order, decree, office copy and other document sealed with the seal of the court	0 50
190.	On the hearing of every case	2 00
191.	On the hearing of every appeal from the registrar or deputy registrar.	2 00
	When judge or surrogate on final disposition of action, orders only half costs under section 257, then one-half of fees to be allowed under this head.	

APPENDIX.

[ADDITIONAL FORMS.]

PLEADINGS.

Adapted from Forms referred to in Sec. 64 of the Rules, viz: those of the Supreme Court of Judicature, and the Vice-Admiralty Courts. Certain of the Forms are given almost in their entirety, as they appear in the Appendix to the V. A. Rules. Others are added.

(1)

Action for damage by collision:

STATEMENT OF CLAIM.

In the Maritime Court of Ontario.

No.... [*Title of Action.*]

Writ issued 18 .

1. Shortly before o'clock on the of January, 18 , the ship *A.B.* of tons register, of which the Plaintiff, *C.D.*, was then owner, whilst on a voyage from to , laden with coals, and manned with a crew of hands, all told, was about miles (*bearing*) from the Light.

2. The wind at that time was about E.N.E., a moderate breeze, the weather was fine, but slightly hazy, and the tide was about slack water, and of little force (*or as the case may be*). The *A.B.* was sailing under all plain sail, close hauled on the port tack, heading about S.E., and proceeding through the water at the rate of about five knots per hour. Her proper regulation side sailing lights were duly placed and exhibited and burning brightly, and a good look-out was being kept on board of her.

3. At that time those on board the *A.B.* observed the red light of a sailing vessel, which proved to be the *X.Y.* at the distance of about from one mile and a half to two miles from the *A.B.*, and bearing about one point on her port bow. The *A.B.* was kept close hauled by the wind on the port tack. The *X.Y.* exhibited her green light and shut in her red light, and drew a little on to the starboard bow of the *A.B.*, and she was then seen to be approaching and causing immediate danger of collision. The helm of the *A.B.* was thereupon put hard down, but the *X.Y.* although loudly hailed from the *A.B.* ran against and with her stem and starboard bow struck the starboard quarter of the *A.B.* abaft the main rigging, and did her so much damage that the *A.B.* soon afterwards sank, and was with her cargo wholly lost, and four of her hands were drowned.

4. There was no proper look-out kept on board the *X.Y.*

5. Those on board the *X.Y.* improperly neglected to take in due time proper measures for avoiding a collision with the *A.B.*

6. The helm of the *X.Y.* was ported at an improper time.

7. The said collision, and the damages and losses consequent thereon, were occasioned by the negligent and improper navigation of those on board the *X.Y.*

The Plaintiff claims—

1. A declaration that he is entitled to the damage proceeded for.
2. The condemnation of the Defendants (and their bail) in such damage and in costs.
3. To have an account taken of such damage with the assistance of merchants.
4. Such further or other relief as the nature of the case may require.

Dated the day of 18 .

(Signed)

Delivered the day of 18 , by (*address in full*), Solicitors for the, &c.

---

(2)

DEFENCE AND COUNTER-CLAIM.

In the Maritime Court of Ontario.

[*Title of Action.*]

1. The Defendants are the owners of the ship *X.Y.* of tons register, carrying a crew of hands all told, and at the time of the circumstances herein-after stated bound on a voyage to

2. A little before o'clock of the , the *X.Y.* was about miles S.E. by S. of the . The wind was E.N.E. The weather was hazy. The *X.Y.* under foresail, fore and main topsails, main topgallant sail, and jib, was heading about W.S.W., making from five to six knots an hour with her regulation light duly exhibited and burning, and a good look-out being kept on board her.

3. In these circumstances, the red lights of two vessels were observed pretty close together, about half mile off, and from two to three points on the starboard bow. The helm of the *X.Y.* was put to port in order to pass on the port sides of these vessels. One, however, of the vessels, which was the *A.B.* altered her course, and exhibited her green light, and caused danger of collision. The helm of the *X.Y.* was then ordered to be steadied, but before this order could be completed was put hard-a-port. The *A.B.* with her starboard side by the main rigging, struck the stem of the *X.Y.* and shortly afterwards sank, her master and four of her crew being saved by the *X.Y.*

4. Save as is herein-before admitted, the several statements in the statement of claim are denied.

5. The *A.B.* was not kept on her course as required by law.

6. The helm of the *A.B.* was improperly starboarded.

7. The collision was caused by one or both of the things stated in the fifth and sixth paragraphs hereof, or otherwise by the negligence of the Plaintiffs, or of those on board the A. B.

8. The collision was not caused or contributed to by the Defendants, or by any of those on board the X. Y.

And by way of Counter-claim, the Defendants say—

They have suffered great damage by reason of the collision.

And they claim as follows—

1. **Judgment against the Plaintiff (and his bail) for the damage occasioned to the Defendants by the collision, and for the costs of this action.**
2. **To have an account taken of such damage with the assistance of merchants.**
3. **Such further and other relief as the nature of the case may require.**

Dated, *etc.*, [*termination as before.*]

(3)

REPLY.

In the Maritime Court of Ontario.

[*Title of Action.*]

The Plaintiff denies the several statements contained in the statement of defence and Counter-claim, *or* admits the several statements contained in paragraphs and of the statement of defence and Counter-claim, but denies the other statements contained therein *or* joins issue upon, &c.

Dated, *etc.*, [*termination.*]

(4)

Action for Salvage:

STATEMENT OF CLAIM.

In the Maritime Court of Ontario:

No.... [*Title of Action.*]

Writ issued 18 .

1. The "Asia" is an iron screw steam ship of tons net register tonnage, fitted with engines of horse-power nominal, is of the value of $———, and was at the time of the services herein-after stated manned with a crew of hands under the command of , her master.

2. At about 9 a.m. on the day of , while the Asia —which was in ballast proceeding on a voyage to to load a cargo of grain—was between and , those on board her saw a steam ship ashore on a bank situated about ten miles to the westward of . The "Asia" immediately steamed in the direction of the distressed vessel which made signals for assistance.

3. On nearing the distressed vessel, which proved to be the "Crosby," one of the "Asia's" boats was sent to the "Crosby," in charge of the second mate of the "Asia," and subsequently the master of the "Crosby" boarded the "Asia," and at the request of the master of the "Crosby" the master of the "Asia" agreed to endeavour to tow the "Crosby" afloat.

4. The "Crosby" at this time was fast aground, and was lying with her head about N.N.W.

5. The master of the "Asia" having ascertained from the master of the "Crosby" the direction in which the "Crosby" had got upon the bank, the "Asia" steamed up on the starboard side of the "Crosby" and was lashed to her.

6. The "Asia" then set on ahead and attempted to tow the "Crosby" afloat, and so continued towing without effect until the hawser which belonged to the "Asia" broke.

7. The masters of the two vessels being then both agreed in opinion that it would be necessary to lighten the "Crosby" before she could be got afloat, it was arranged that the cargo from the "Crosby" should be taken on board the "Asia."

8. The "Asia" was again secured alongside the "Crosby" and the hatches being taken off cargo was then discharged from the "Crosby" into the "Asia," and this operation was continued until about 6 p.m., by which time about 100 tons of such cargo had been so discharged.

9. When this had been done both vessels used their steam, and the "Asia" tried again to get the "Crosby" off, but without success. The "Asia" then towed with a hawser ahead of the "Crosby," and succeeded in getting her afloat, upon which the "Crosby" steamed to an anchorage and then brought up.

10. The "Asia" steamed after the "Crosby" and again hauled alongside of her and commenced putting the transhipped cargo again on board the "Crosby," and continued doing so until about 6 a.m., of the 30th of April, by which time the operation was completed, and the "Crosby" and her cargo being in safety the "Asia" proceeded on her voyage.

11. By the services of the Plaintiffs the "Crosby" and her cargo were rescued from a very dangerous and critical position, as in the event of bad weather coming on whilst she lay aground she would have been in very great danger of being lost with her cargo.

12. The "Asia" encountered some risk in being lashed alongside the "Crosby," and she ran risk of also getting aground and of losing her charter, the blockade of the port of Nikolaev being at the time imminent.

13. The value of the hawser of the "Asia" broken as herein stated was $.

14. The "Crosby" is an iron screw steam ship of tons net (gross) register tonnage. As salved the "Crosby" and her cargo and freight have been agreed for the purposes of this action at the value of $.

The Plaintiffs claim—

1. Such an amount of salvage, regard being had to the said agreement, as the Court may think fit to award.
2. The condemnation of the Defendants [and their bail] in the salvage and in costs.
3. Such further and other relief as the case may require.

Dated, *etc.*

(5)

DEFENCE.

In the Maritime Court of Ontario.

[*Title of Action.*]

1. The Defendants admit that the statement of facts contained in the statement of claim is substantially correct, except that the re-shipment of the cargo on board the "Crosby" was completed by 4 a.m. on the 30th April.

2. The Defendants submit to the judgment of the Court to award such a moderate amount of salvage to the Plaintiffs under the circumstances aforesaid as to the said court shall seem meet.

[*termination*].

---

(6)

REPLY.

In the Maritime Court of Ontario.

[*Title of Action.*]

The Plaintiffs deny the statement contained in the 1st parapragh of the statement of defence, that the shipment of the cargo was completed by 4 a.m. on the 30th April.

Dated, *etc.*, [*termination*].

---

(7)

(3.) *Action for distribution of salvage:*

STATEMENT OF CLAIM.

In the Maritime Court of Ontario.

[*Title of Action.*]

Writ issued 18 .

1. *Describe briefly the salvage services, stating the part taken in them by the Plaintiffs, and the capacity in which they were serving.*

2. The sum of $ has been paid by the owners of the ship, &c' [*state name of ship or other property solved*] to the Defendants, as owners of the ship [*state name of salving ship*], and has been accepted by them in satisfaction of their claim for salvage, but the said Defendants have not paid and refuse to pay any part of that sum to the Plaintiffs for their share in the said salvage services.

The Plaintiffs claim—

1. An equitable share of the said sum of $, to be apportioned among them as the Court shall think fit and the costs of this action.
2. Such other relief as the nature of the case may require.

Dated, *etc.*

(8)

Action for master's wages and disbursements:

STATEMENT OF CLAIM.

In the Maritime Court of Ontario.

[*Title of Action.*]

Writ issued 18 .

1. The plaintiff, on the 10th day of February 1877, was appointed by the owner of the British barque "Princess," proceeded against in this action, master of the said barque, and it was agreed between the Plaintiff and the said owner that the wages of the Plaintiff as master should he $ per month.

2. The Plaintiff acted as master of the said barque from the said 10th day of February until the 25th day of October 18 , and there is now due to him for his wages as master during that time the sum of $.

3. The plaintiff as master of the said barque expended various sums of money for necessary disbursements on account of the said barque; and there is now due to him in respect of the same a balance of $.

The plaintiff claims—

1. A decree pronouncing the said sums, amounting in the whole to $, to be due to him for wages and disbursements, and directing the said vessel to be sold and the amount due to him to be paid to him out of the proceeds.
2. Such further and other relief as the nature of the case may require.

Dated, *etc.*

---

(9)

Action for Seamen's wages:

STATEMENT OF CLAIM.

In the Maritime Court of Ontario,

[*Title of Action.*]

Writ issued 18—.

1. The Plaintiff, *A.B.*, was engaged as mate of the British brig "Bristol at the rate of $ per month, and in pursuance of that engagement served as mate on board the said brig from the day of 18 , to the day of 18 , and during that time as mate of the said brig earned wages amounting to $. After giving credit for the sum received by him on account, as shown in the schedule hereto, there remains due to him for his wages a balance of $.

2. The plaintiffs *C.D.*, *E.F.*, and *G.H.*, were engaged as able seamen on board the said brig, and having in pursuance of that engagement served as able seamen on board the said brig during the periods specified in the schedule hereto, earned thereby as wages the sums set forth in the same schedule, and after giving credit for the sums received by them respectively, on account of the said wages, there remain due to them the following sums; namely,

To *C.D.*, the sum of $
To *E.F.*, " $
To *G.H.*, " $

3. The plaintiffs *I.K.*, and *L.M.*, were engaged as ordinary seamen on board the said brig, and having served on board the same in pursuance of the said engagement, during the periods specified in the schedule hereto, earned thereby the sums set forth in the same schedule, and after giving credit for the sums received by them respectively, on account of the said wages, there remain due to them the following sums; namely,

To *I.K.* the sum of $.
To *L.M.* " $.

SCHEDULE referred to above.

Wages due *A.B.*, mate, from the 18 , to the 18 , months and days at $ per month.

$

Less received on account......$

Balance due......$

Wages due to *C.D.*, able seaman, from the 18 , to the 18, months and days, at $ per month.

$

Less received on account......$

Balance due......$

[*so on with the wages due to the other plaintiffs*].

The Plaintiffs claim—

1. The several sums so due to them respectively with the costs of this action.
2. Such double pay as they may be entitled to under sec. 187 of the Merchant Shipping Act, 1854 (*a*).
3. Such other relief as the nature of the case may require.

Dated, *etc.*

(*a*) The provision as to 10 days double pay is not contained in the "Inland Waters Seamen's Act."

---

(10)

Action on Mortgage:

STATEMENT OF CLAIM.

In the Maritime Court of Ontario.

[*Title of Action.*]

Writ issued 18 .

1. The above-named or vessel is a British ship belonging to the port of , of the registered tonnage of tons or thereabouts, and at the time of the mortgage here-inafter mentioned, , of , was the registered owner of the said vessel.

2. On the day of , 64th parts or shares of the said vessel were mortgaged by the said to the Plaintiff, to secure the payment by the said to the Plaintiff of the sum of $, together with interest thereon at the rate of per cent. per annum on or before the day of 18 ,

3. The said mortgage of the said vessel was made by an instrument dated the day of 18 , in the form prescribed by the 66th section of the Merchant Shipping Act, 1854, and was duly registered in accordance with the provisions of the said Act.

4. No part of the said principal sum or interest has been paid, and there still remains due and owing to the Plaintiff on the said mortgage security the principal sum of $, together with a large sum of money for interest and expenses, and the Plaintiff, although he has applied to the said for payment thereof, cannot obtain payment without the assistance of this Court.

The Plaintiff claims—

1. Judgment for the said principal sum of $, together with interest and expenses.
2. To have an account taken of the amount due to the Plaintiff.
3. Payment out of the proceeds of the said vessel now remaining in Court, of the amount found due to the Plaintiff, together with costs.
4. Such further and other relief as the nature of the case may require.

Dated, etc.

---

(11)

Action on Mortgage

STATEMENT OF CLAIM.

In the Maritime Court of Ontario.

[*Title of Action.*]

1. By an indenture dated the day of , made between one *A.B.*, then being the sole owner of the steamship Empress, registered at the Port of in the Province of Ontario, (*a*) of the one part, and the Plaintiff of the other part; the said *A.B.* in consideration of the sum of $, paid to him by the Plaintiff, conveyed to the Plaintiff 64-64th shares in the said ship subject to a proviso for the redemption of the same on payment by the said *A. B.*, his executors, administrators or assigns, to the Plaintiff of the sum of $ with interest for the same at the rate of per cent. per annum on the day of then next ensuing.

2. The whole of the said sum of $ with an arrear of interest thereon remains due to the Plaintiff on his said security.

The Plaintiff claims—

1. Judgment giving possession of the said ship to the Plaintiff.
2. The condemnation of the Defendant in the costs of the action.
3. Such further or other relief as the nature of the case may require

Dated, etc.

(*a*) See *ante*, p. 6.

(12)

Action between co-owners (for account):

STATEMENT OF CLAIM.

In the Maritime Court of Ontario.

[*Title of Action.*]

Writ issued 18 .

1. The "Horlock" is a sailing ship of about 40 tons register, trading between and .

2. By a bill of sale duly registered on the 11th day of June 18 , the Defendant, John Horlock, who was then sole owner of the above named ship "Horlock" transferred to Thomas Warraker, of , 32-64th parts or shares of the ship for the sum of $.

3. By a subsequent bill of sale duly registered on the 16th December 18 , the said Thomas Worraker transferred his said 32-64th shares of the ship to George Wright, the Plaintiff, for the sum of $.

4. The Defendant, John Horlock, has had the entire management and the command of the said ship from the 11th day of June, 18 down to the present time.

5. The Defendant has from time to time up to and including the 24th September 18 , rendered accounts of the earnings of the ship to the afore-mentioned Thomas Worraker, but since the said 24th September 18 the Defendant has rendered no accounts of the earnings of the ship.

6. Since the 16th December 18 the ship has continued to trade between and , and the Plaintiff has made several applications to the Defendant, John Horlock, for an account of the earnings of the ship, but such applications have proved ineffectual.

7. The Plaintiff is dissatisfied with the management of the ship, and consequently desires that she may be sold.

The Plaintiff claims—

1. That the court may direct the sale of the ship "Horlock."
2. To have an account taken of the earnings of the said ship, and that the Defendant be condemned in the amount which shall be found due to the Plaintiff in respect thereof, and in the costs of this action.
3. Such further or other relief as the nature of the case may require.

Dated, etc,

(13.)

DEFENCE.

In the Maritime Court of Ontario.

[*Title of Action.*]

1. The Defendant denies the statements contained in paragraph 2 of the petition.

2. The Defendant further says that he never at any time signed any bill of sale transferring any shares whatever of the said ship "Horlock" to the said Thomas Worraker, and further says that if any such bill was

registered as alleged on the 11th June in the said 2nd paragraph (which the Defendant denies) the same was made and registered fraudulently and without the knowledge, consent, or authority of the Defendant.

3. The Defendant does not admit the statements contained in the 3rd paragraph of the petition. and says that if the said Thomas Worraker transferred any shares of the said ship to the Plaintiff as alleged (which the defendant does not admit), he did so wrongfully and unlawfully, and that he had not possession of or any right to or in respect of the said shares.

4. The Defendant denies the statements contained in paragraph 5 of the petition, and says that he never rendered any such accounts as alleged therein.

5. The Defendant does not admit the statements contained in paragraph 6 of the petition.

Dated, *etc.*

---

(14)

REPLY.

In the Maritime Court of Ontario.

[*Title of Action.*]

The Plaintiff denies the several statements contained in the Defendant's statement of defence.

Dated, *etc.*

---

(15)

In an action for possession.

Statement of Claim.

In the Maritime Court of Ontario,

[*Title of Action.*]

Writ issued 18 .

1. The Plaintiffs are registered owners of 44-64th shares in the British ship "Native Pearl," and such shares are held by them respectively as follows:—

Morgan Parsall Griffiths is owner of 16-64th shares, Edmund Nicholls of 8-64th shares, William Meager of 4-64th shares, Isaac Butler of 8-64th shares, and William Herbert of 8-64th shares.

2. The only owner of the said ship other than the plaintiffs is John Nicholas Richardson, who is the registered owner of the remaining 20-64th shares of this ship, and has hitherto acted as managing owner and ship's husband of the said ship, and has possession of and control over the said ship and her certificate of registry.

3. The defendant the said John Nicholas Richardson, has not managed the said ship to the satisfaction of the plaintiffs, and has, by his management of her occasioned, great loss to the plaintiffs; and the plaintiffs in consequence thereof before the commencement of this action gave notice to the defendant to cease acting as as managing owner and ship's husband of the said ship and revoked his authority in that behalf, and demanded from the defendant the possession and control of the said ship and of her certificate of registry, but the defen-

dant has refused to give possession of the said ship and certificate to the plaintiffs, and the plaintiffs cannot obtain possession of them without the assistance of this Court.

4. The defendant has neglected and refused to render proper accounts relating to the management and earnings of the said ship and such, accounts are still outstanding and unsettled between the plaintiffs and the defendant.

The plaintiffs claim—

1. Judgment giving possession to the plaintiffs of the said ship and of her certificate of registry.

2. To have an account taken, with the assistance of merchants, of the earnings of the ship.

3. A sale of the defendant's shares in the said ship.

4. Payment out of the proceeds of such sale of the balance (if any) found due to the plaintiffs and of the costs of this action.

5. Such further and other relief as the nature as the case may require.

Dated, *etc.*

---

(16)

Action for Necessaries:

STATEMENT OF CLAIM.

In the Maritime Court of Ontario.

[*Title of Action.*]

Writ issued 18 .

1. The Plaintiffs at the time of the occurrences hereinafter mentioned carried on business at the port of as bonded store and provision merchants and ship chandlers.

2. The "Sfactoria" is a Greek ship, [*or* a ship of the United States of America, as the case may be] and in the months of June, July, August, and September 18 was lying in the said port of under the command of one George Lazzaro, a foreigner, her master and owner, and in the said month of September she proceeded on her voyage to .

3. The plaintiffs, at the request and by the direction of the said master, supplied during the said months of June, July, August, and September 18 , stores and other necessaries for the necessary use of the said ship upon the said then intended voyage to the value of $, for which sum an acceptance was given by the said George Lazzaro to the Plaintiffs; but on the 4th day of February 18 , the said acceptance, which then became due, was dishonoured, and the said sum of $ with interest thereon from the 4th day of February 18 , still remains due and unpaid to the Plaintiffs.

4. In the month of August aforesaid the plaintiffs, at the request of the said master, advanced to him the sum of $ for the necessary disbursements of the said ship at the said port of , and otherwise on account of the said ship; and also at his request paid the sum of $ which was due for goods supplied for the necessary use of the said ship

on the said voyage; and of the sums so advanced and paid there still remains due and unpaid to the plaintiffs the sum of $, with interest thereon from the 6th day of January 18 , on which last-mentioned day a promissory note given by the said George Lazzaro to the said plaintiffs for the sum said of $ was returned to them dishonoured.

5. The Plaintiffs also at the said master's request, between the 1st of September 18 and the commencment of this action paid various sums amounting to $ for the insurance of their said debt.

6, The said goods were supplied and the said sums advanced and paid by the Plaintiffs upon the credit of the said ship, and not merely on the personal credit of the said master.

The Plaintiff's claim—

1. Judgment for the said sums of $, and $, together with interest thereon.
2. That the Defendant (and his bail) be condemned therein, and in costs;

or

2 A sale of the said ship, and payment of the said sums and interest out of the proceeds of such sale, together with costs.

3. Such further and other relief as the case may require.

Dated, *etc.*

---

(17)

Towage.

STATEMENT OF CLAIM.

In the Maritime Court of Ontario.

[*Title of Action.*]

1. On the day of the ship Three Brothers, whereof the Defendants are the owners, arrived off Gibralter Point, and here the master of the said ship agreed to engage the steam-tug Robb, whereof the Plaintiffs are the owners, to tow the said ship into the harbour of Toronto, and to dock or wharf for reward in that behalf.

2. The Robb took the said ship in tow, and continued in charge of her until she was placed in the said dock.

3. For the said services so rendered to the said ship as aforesaid, there is due to the Plaintiffs the said sum of $.

4- The Defendants have refused to pay the said sum of $ and the same is still due and owing to the Plaintiffs.

The Plaintiffs claim—

1. Judgment pronouncing for the claim of the Plaintiffs.
2. The condemnation of the Defendants, and their bail in the costs of this action.
3. Such further or other relief as the case may require.

Dated, *etc.*

(18)

ORDER CONSOLIDATING ACTIONS.

In the Maritime Court of Ontario.

No. [*Title of Action.*]

Upon the application of the in action number (*or as the case may be*), and upon reading the certificate of the registrar of this court, whereby it appears that actions numbers and are for wages, and it appearing also that the said action number is also for wages, and is instituted in the same office (*or the case may be*) and against the same property as the said other action. And the plaintiffs in said action number , undertaking that all proceedings to be taken therein shall apply to and include the said action number , and that the decree in the said action number shall include all necessary provisions and directions for the benefit of the plaintiff in said action number and for realizing the amount which may be ascertained to be due to for said claims and costs. And upon hearing for the in said actions, it is ordered that all further proceedings in said action number be stayed and that the same be consolidated with the said action number and that the said last named action be proceeded with against said property on behalf of all said plaintiffs.

Dated at Chambers. } Judge.

---

(19)

BOND FOR SECURITY FOR COSTS ON APPEAL TO SUPREME COURT OF CANADA.

In the Maritime Court of Ontario.

No. [*Title of Action.*]

Required by Sec. 46, "*Supreme and Exchequer Courts' Act.*"

KNOW ALL MEN by these presents that we, *A.B.*, of the of in the county of , and Province of , *C.D.* of , and *E.F.* of , are jointly and severally held, and jointly bound unto *G.H.* in the penal sum of five hundred dollars, for which payment well and truly to be made, we bind ourselves and each of us by himself, our and each of our heirs, executors, and administrators, firmly by these presents. Dated this day of A.D. 18 .

Whereas a certain action was brought in the Maritime Court of Ontario at , by the said *A.B.* as plaintiff against . And whereas a judgment or decision was pronounced by the judge of the said court (*or* by the Surrogate judge of the said court at) and a decree (*or order*) was made in said action on the day of (*or as the case may be*) against the said . And whereas the said complains that in pronouncing the said judgment in said action, manifest error hath intervened, wherefore the said desires to appeal from the said judgment decision, decree, or order (*or as the case may be*) to the Supreme Court of Canada.

Now the condition of this obligation is such, that if the said shall effectually prosecute his said appeal and pay such costs and damages as may be awarded against him by the Supreme Court of Canada, then this obligation shall be void, otherwise to remain in full force and effect.

Signed, sealed, and delivered in presence of,	*A.B.*	L.S.
	C.D.	L.S.
	E.F.	L.S.

---

(20)

AFFIDAVIT OF EXECUTION.

In the Maritime Court of Ontario.

[*Title of Action.*]

The .

I, , of the , make oath and say (1) that I was personally present and did see the foregoing instrument duly signed, sealed, and executed by parties thereto.

(2) That the said instrument was executed at .

(3) That I know the said parties,

(4) That I am a subscribing witness to the said instrument.

Sworn before me at the
of
in the county of
this day of 18 .

---

(21)

AFFIDAVIT OF JUSTIFICATION.

In the Maritime Court of Ontario.

[*Title of Action.*]

No. . The .

I, *C.D.*, of , make oath and say, that I am a resident inhabitant of the Province of , and am a freeholder in the of aforesaid, and that I am worth the sum of $1,000 over and above what will pay all my debts.

And I, the said *E.F.*, of the of , make oath and say, that I am a resident inhabitant of the said Province of , and am a freeholder in the of aforesaid, and that I am worth the sum of $1,000, over and above what will pay my debts.

The above named deponents, *C.D.* and *E.F.*, were severally sworn before me in the of in the county of and Province of this day of 18 .	*C.D.* *E.F.*

(22)

POWER OF ATTORNEY TO RECEIVE MONEY.

In the Maritime Court of Ontario.

No . [*Title of Action.*]

I, of State of , one of of the United States of America, (*or as the case may be*), do hereby appoint and authorise of the of in the Province of Ontario , as my Attorney, to receive for me all sums of money which may be payable to me out of the proceeds arising from the sale of the said vessel, remaining in court decreed or awarded to me in the said action, (*or as the case may be*), and in my name to give all necessary receipts and acquittances for the same.

In witness whereof I have hereunto set my hand and seal this day of 18 .

Signed, sealed, and delivered in presence of } L.S.

[*Add Affidavit of Execution as Form (20)*]

INLAND WATERS SEAMEN'S ACT.

Revised Statutes of Canada, Chapter 75.

An Act respecting the Shipping of Seamen on Inland Waters, A.D. 1886 (referred to in preceding Rules.)

HER Majesty, by and with the advice and consent of the Senate and House of Commons of Canada, enacts as follows:—

SHORT TITLE.

Short title.

1. This Act may be cited as "*The Inland Waters Seamen's Act.*" 38 V., c. 29, s. 1.

INTERPRETATION.

Interpretation.

2. In this Act, unless the context otherwise requires,—

"Ship."

(*a.*) The expression "ship" includes every description of vessel used in navigation, not propelled by oars;

"Master."

(*b.*) The expression "master" includes every person having command or charge of a ship, except a pilot;

"Seaman."

(*c*) The expression "seaman" includes every person employed or engaged in any capacity on board any ship, except masters and pilots;

"Consular Officer."

(*d.*) The expression "Consular officer" includes Consul General, Consul, and Vice-Consul, and any person for the time being discharing the duties of Consul General, Consul or Vice-Consul.

"Minister."

(*e.*) The expression "the Minister" means the Minister of of Marine and Fisheries;

"Ship subject to the provisions of this Act.

(*f.*) The expression "ship subject to the provisions of this Act" includes every ship registered in Canada propelled by steam, and of more than twenty tons, registered tonnage, or propelled otherwise than by steam, and of more than fifty tons registered tonnage, and employed in navigating the inland waters of Canada above the harbor of Quebec. 38 V., c. 29, s. 2, *part.*

APPLICATION OF ACT.

Act not to apply to barges, &c.

3. This Act shall not apply to barges and scows navigating rivers and canals. 38 V., c. 29, s. 2, *part.*

ENGAGEMENT AND WAGES OF SEAMEN.

Agreement between master and crew.

Form of agreement.

4. The master of every ship subject to the provisions of this Act, shall enter into an agreement with every seamen whom he carries as one of his crew, in the manner hereinafter mentioned; and every such agreement shall be in the form of the schedule to this Act, or as near thereto as circumstances admit, and shall be dated at the time of the first signature thereof, and shall be signed by the master before any seaman signs the same, and shall contain the following particulars as terms thereof, that is to say:—

Particulars.

(*a.*) The nature and, as far as practicable, the duration of the intended voyage or engagement;

Nature of voyage.

(*b.*) The number and description of the crew, specifying how many are engaged as sailors;

Crew.

(*c.*) The time at which each seamen is to be on board or to begin work:

Time for work.

(*d.*) The capacity in which each seaman is to serve;

Capacity.

(*e.*) The amount of wages which each seaman is to receive;

Wages.

(*f.*) Any regulations as to conduct on board, and as to fines, or other lawful punishments for misconduct which the parties agree to adopt:

Conduct, &c.

2. Every such agreement shall be so framed as to admit of stipulations, to be adopted at the will of the master and seamen in each case, as to advances, and may contain any other stipulations which are not contrary to law; and every such agreement shall be made and signed in presence of a respectable witness, or a shipping master or chief officer of customs, who shall attest each signature on such agreement;

To be so framed as to admit of certain stipulations.

3. Any seaman who has signed any such agreement may, at the termination of his engagement, if the master thinks fit, be discharged before any shipping master or chief officer of customs in Canada; and at any period during any such engagement, and before its termination, the master may discharge any such seaman on payment of his wages, and with his consent, and any such discharge may be made, if the master thinks fit, before any shipping master or chief officer of customs in Canada. 38 V., c. 29, s. 3.

Discharge of seamen, how effected.

5. In the case of ships subject to the provisions of this Act making short voyages, running agreements with the crew may be made to extend over two or more voyages, or for a specified time, so that no such agreement shall extend beyond eight months from the date of such agreement, or the first arrival of the ship at her port of destination after the termination of such agreement, or the discharge of cargo consequent upon such arrival; and every person entering into such agreement, whether engaged upon the first commencement thereof, or otherwise, shall enter into and sign the same in the manner hereinbefore required; and every person engaged thereunder when discharged may be discharged in the manner hereinbefore provided for. 38 V., c. 29, s. 4.

Duration of agreement.

Engagement and discharge.

6. Every master of any ship subject to the provisions of this Act, who carries any seaman as one of his crew without entering into an agreement with him, in the form and manner and at the place and time in such case required, shall, for each such offence, incur a penalty not exceeding twenty dollars. 38 V., c. 29, s.

Penalty for carrying seamen without agreement.

7. Every erasure, interlineation or alteration in any such agreement with seamen as is required by this Act, except additions made for shipping substitutes or persons engaged subsequently to the first departure of the ship, shall be wholly inoperative, unless proved to have been made with the consent of all the persons interested in such erasure, interlineation or alteration,

Erasures, &c. in agreement void, unless consent of all parties is proved.

by the written attestation, if made in Her Majesty's Dominions, of some shipping master, justice of the peace, officer of customs or other public functionary, or, if made out of Her Majesty's Dominions, of a British consular officer, or where there is no such officer, of two respectable witnesses. 38 V., c. 29, s. 6.

Penalty for fraudulently altering agreement, &c.

8. Every person who fraudulently alters, assists in fraudulently altering, or procures to be fraudulently altered, or makes or assists in making or procures to be made, any false entry in, or delivers, assists in delivering, or procures to be delivered a false copy of any agreement under this Act, is guilty of a misdemeanour, 38 V., c. 29, s. 7.

Proof of agreement.

9. Any seaman may bring forward evidence to prove the contents of any agreement under this Act or otherwise to support his case, without producing or giving notice to produce the agreement or any copy thereof. 38 V., c. 29, s. 8.

Right of seaman discharged without cause before the end of his term of agreement.

10. Any seaman who has signed an agreement under this Act, and is afterwards discharged before the commencement of the voyage, or before one month's wages are earned, without fault on his part justifying such discharge and without his consent, shall be entitled to receive from the master or owner, in addition to any wages he has earned, due compensation for the damage thereby caused to him,—not exceeding one month's wages; and may, on adducing such evidence as the court hearing the case deems satisfactory of his having been so improperly discharged, recover such compensation as if it were wages duly earned. 38 V., c. 29, s. 9.

Attestation of agreement or discharge and fee to officers.

11. Whenever any agreement under this Act is signed before any shipping master or a chief officer of customs as a witness thereto, such officer shall append his title of office to his signature as such witness; and the sum of forty cents shall be payable to every such officer upon each engagement of a seaman before him, and the sum of twenty cents shall be payable to every such officer upon each discharge of a seaman effected before him as hereinbefore mentioned; and any shipping master or chief officer of customs may refuse to sign any such engagement or discharge, as a witness thereto, unless the fee payable thereon is first paid. 38 V., c. 29, s. 10.

As to seaman whose term of service is terminated without his fault.

12. Whenever the service of any seaman belonging to any ship subject to the provisions of this Act, terminates before the period contemplated in the agreement, by reason of the wreck or loss of the ship, and whenever such service terminates before such period as aforesaid, by reason of his being left on shore at any place abroad, under a certificate of his unfitness or inability to proceed on the voyage, granted by competent authority, such seaman shall be entitled to wages for the time of service prior to such termination as aforesaid, but not for any further period. 38 V., c. 29, s. 11.

Seaman unlawfully refusing to work, &c.

13. No seaman belonging to any ship subject to the provisions of this Act, shall be entitled to wages for any period during which he unlawfully refuses or neglects to work when required, whether before or after the time fixed by the agreement for his beginning work, or, unless the court hearing the case otherwise directs, for any period during which he is lawfully imprisoned for any offence committed by him. 38 V., c. 29, s. 12.

14. Whenever a seaman belonging to any ship subject to the provisions of this Act, is, by reason of illness, incapable of performing his duty, and it is proved that such illness has been caused by his own wilful act or default, he shall not be entitled to wages for the time during which he is, by reason of such illness, incapable of performing his duty. 38 V., c. 29, s. 13. **Seaman disabled by illness caused by his own wilful act.**

15. No seaman belonging to any ship subject to the provisions of this Act, who is engaged for a voyage or engagement which is to terminate in Canada, shall be entitled to sue in any court out of Canada for wages, unless he is discharged with the written consent of the master or proves such ill-usage on the part of the master or by his authority, as to warrant reasonable apprehension of danger to the life of such seaman if he remained on board; but if any seaman, on his return to Canada, proves that the master or owner has been guilty of any conduct or default which, but for this section, would have entitled the seaman to sue for wages before the termination of the voyage or engagement, he shall be entitled to recover, in addition to his wages, such compensation; not exceeding eighty dollars, as the court hearing the case thinks reasonable. 38 V., c. 29, s. 14. **Seaman not to sue for wages in court out of Canada, except in certain cases.** **Proviso.**

16. The master or owner of every ship subject to the provisions of this Act shall, at all times when required so to do by the Minister or by any person in that behalf duly authorized by the Minister, or by any inspector of steamboats or custom house officer or officer of river police, produce and exhibit to the Minister or to such person authorized by him, or to such inspector of steamboats or custom house officer or officer of river police, any agreement then in force and subsisting between the master of such ship and the seamen whom he carries as his crew; and every such owner or master who fails to comply with the requirements of this section shall incur a penalty of twenty dollars. 38. V., c. 29, s. 15. **Master or owner bound to produce agreement to certain officers.** **Penalty for default.**

DISCIPLINE.

17. Every master of and every seaman belonging to any ship subject to the provisions of this Act, who, by wilful breach of duty, or by neglect of duty, or by reason of drunkenness, does any act tending to the immediate loss, destruction or serious damage of such ship, or tending immediately to endanger the life or limb of any person belonging to or on board of such ship, or who, by wilful breach of duty, or by neglect of duty, or by reason of drunkenness, refuses or omits to do any lawful act, proper and requisite to be done by him for preserving such ship from immediate loss, destruction or serious damage, or for preserving any person belonging to or on board of such ship from immediate danger to life or limb, is guilty of a misdemeanor. 38 V., c. 29, s. 16. **Misconduct endangering ship, life or limb a misdemeanor.**

Offences of seamen and their punishment.

18. Whenever any seaman, who has been lawfully engaged or bound to any ship subject to the provisions of this Act, and has duly signed an agreement as required by this Act, commits any of the following offences, he shall be liable to be punished summarily as follows, that is to say:

Desertion.

(*a.*) For desertion, he shall be liable to imprisonment for any term not exceeding twelve weeks and not less than four weeks, with hard labor, and also to forfeit all or any part of the clothes and effects he leaves on board, and all or any part of the wages or emoluments which he has then earned, and also, if such desertion takes place abroad, at the discretion of the court, to forfeit all or any part of the wages or emoluments earned in any other ship in which he is employed until his next return to Canada, and to satisfy any excess of wages paid by the master or owner of the ship from which he deserts to any substitute engaged in his place at a higher rate of wages than the rate stipulated to be paid to him;

Neglecting or refusing to join ship or proceed on voyage.

Absence without leave.

(*b.*) For neglecting or refusing, without reasanable cause, to join his ship, or to proceed on any voyage in his ship, or for absence without leave at any time within twenty-four hours of the ship's sailing from any port, either at the commencement or during the progress of any voyage, or for absence at any time without leave and without sufficient reason from his ship or from his duty, not amounting to desertion or not treated as such by the master, he shall be liable to imprisonment for any term not exceeding ten weeks and not less than four weeks, with or without hard labor, and also, in the discretion of the court, to forfeit out of his wages a sum not exceeding the amount of two days' pay, and in addition, for every twenty-four hours of absence, either a sum not exceeding six days' pay, or any expenses which have been properly incurred in hiring a substitute;

Quitting without leave, before ship is secured.

(*c.*) For quitting the ship without leave after after her arrival in her port of delivery, and before she is placed in security, he shall be liable to forfeit out of his wages a sum not exceeding one month's pay;

Act of willful disobedience.

(*d.*) For willful disobedience to any lawful command he shall be liable to imprisonment for any term not exceeding four weeks and not less that two weeks, with or without hard labour, and also, at the discretion of the court, to forfeit out of his wages a sum not exceeding two days' pay;

Continued disobedience or neglect of duty.

(*e.*) For continued willful disobedience to lawful commands, or continued willful neglect of duty, he shall be liable to imprisonment for any term not exceeding twelve weeks and not less than four weeks, with or without hard labour, and also, in the discretion of the court, to forfeit, for every twenty-four hours' continuance of such disobedience or neglect, either a sum not exceeding six days' pay, or the amount of any expenses which have been properly incurred in hiring a substitute;

Assault on officers of ship.

(*f.*) For assaulting any master or mate, he shall be liable to imprisonment for any term not exceeding twelve weeks and not less than six weeks, with hard labour;

Combining to disobey or neglect duty.

(*g.*) For combining with any other or others of the crew to disobey lawful commands, or to neglect duty, or to impede the navigation of the ship or the progress of the voyage, he shall be liable to imprisonment, with hard labour, for any term not exceeding twelve weeks and not less than six weeks;

(*h.*) For wilfully damaging the ship, or embezzling or wilfully damaging any of her stores or cargo, he shall be liable to forfeit out of his wages a sum equal in value to the loss thereby sustained, and also, in the discretion of the court, to imprisonment, with hard labour, for any term not exceeding twelve weeks and not less than six weeks; Wilful damage or embezzlement.

(*i.*) For any act of smuggling of which he is convicted, and whereby loss or damage is occasioned to the master or owner, he shall be liable to pay to such master or owner such a sum as is sufficient to reimburse the master or owner for such loss or damage; and the whole or a proportionate part of his wages may be retained in satisfaction or on account of such liability, without prejudice to any further remedy. 38 V. c. 29, s. 17. Act of smuggling causing loss to owner.

19. Whenever, either at the commencement or during the progress of any voyage, any seaman negletcs or refuses to proceed in any ship subject to the provisions of this Act, in which he is duly engaged to serve, or is found otherwise absenting himself therefrom without leave, the master or any mate, or the owner, ship's husband or consignee may, in any place in Canada, with or without the assistance of the local police officers or constables (who shall give the same if required) apprehend him without first procuring a warrant—and may thereupon in any case, and shall, in case he so requires and it is practicable, convey him before some court capable of taking cognizance of the matter, to be dealt with according to law, and may, for the purpose of conveying him before such court, detain him in custody for a period not exceeding twenty-four hours, or such shorter time as is necessary, or may, if he does not so require, or if there is no such court at or near the place, at once convey him on board; and if any such apprehension appears to the court before which the case is brought to have been made on improper or on insufficient grounds, the master, mate, owner, ship's husband or consignee who makes the same or causes the same to be made, shall incur a penalty not exceeding eighty dollars; but such penalty, if inflicted, shall be a bar to any action for false imprisonment in respect of such apprehension. 38 V., c. 29, s. 18. Master or owner may apprehend deserters without warrant. Penalty for improper arrest.

20. Whenever any seaman belonging to any ship subject to the provisions of this Act, is brought before any court in Canada on the ground of his having neglected or refused to join or proceed in any ship in which he is engaged to serve, or of having deserted or otherwise absented himself therefrom without leave, such court may,—if the master or the owner or his agent so requires,—instead of commiting the offender to prison, cause him to proceed on board for the purpose of proceeding on the voyage, or deliver him to the master or any mate of the ship, or owner or his agent, to be by him so conveyed, and may, in such case, order any costs and expenses properly incurred by or on behalf of the master or owner by reason of the offence, to be paid by the offender, and, if necessary, to be deducted from any wages which he has then earned, or which, by virtue of his then existing engagement, he afterwards earns. 38 V. c. 29, s. 19. Deserters may be sent on board in lieu of being imprisoned.

21. If any seaman is imprisoned on the ground of his having neglected or refused to join or to proceed in any ship subject to the Seamen imprisoned for desertion or or breach of discipline may be sent on board before termination of sentence.

provisions of this Act, in which he is engaged to serve, or of his having deserted or otherwise absented himself therefrom without leave, or of his having committed any other breach of discipline, and if, during such imprisonment, and belore his engagement is at an end, his services are required on board his ship, any justice of the peace may, at the request of the master or of the owner or his agent, cause such seaman to be conveyed on board his said ship for the purpose of proceeding on the voyage, or to be delivered to the master or any mate of the ship, or to the owner or his agent, to be by him so conveyed, notwithstanding that the termination of the period for which he was sentenced to imprisonment has not arrived. 38 V., c.29, s. 20.

Facilities for proving desertion, so far as concerns forfeiture of wages.

22. Whenever the question arises whether the wages of any seaman belonging to any ship subject to the provisions of this Act, are forfeited for desertion, it shall be sufficient for the person insisting on the forfeiture to show that such seaman was duly engaged in or that he belonged to the ship from which he is alleged to have deserted, and that he quitted such ship before the completion of the voyage or engagement; and thereupon the desertion shall, so far as relates to any forfeiture of wages or emoluments under the provisions hereinbefore contained, be deemed to be proved, unless the seaman can produce a proper certificate of discharge, or can otherwise show, to the satisfaction of the court, that he had sufficient reasons for leaving his ship. 38 V., c. 29, s, 21.

Cost of procuring imprisonment may, to the extent of $12, be deducted from wages.

23. Whenever, in any proceeding relating to seamen's wages, it is shown that any seaman belonging to any ship subject to the provisions of this Act, has, in the course of the voyage, been convicted of any offence by any competent tribunal, and rightfully punished therefor by imprisonment or otherwise, the court hearing the case may direct a part of the wages due to such seaman, not exceeding twelve dollars, to be applied in reimbursing any costs properly incurred by the master in procuring such conviction or punishment. 38 V., c. 29, s. 22.

Amount of forfeiture how to be ascertained when seamen contract for the voyage.

24. Whenever any seaman belonging to any ship subject to the provisions of this Act, contracts for wages by the voyage, or by the run or by the share, and not by the month or other stated period of time,the amount of forfeiture to be incurred under this Act shall be taken to be an amount bearing the same proportion to the whole wages or share, as a month or other the period hereinbefore mentioned in fixing the amount of such forfeiture, as the case may be, bears to the whole time spent in the voyage; and if the whole time spent in the voyage does not exceed the the period for which the pay is to be forfeited, the forfeiture shall extend to the wages or share. 38 V., c. 29, s. 23.

Application of forfeitures.

25. All clothes, effects, wages and emoluments which under the provisions hereinbefore contained, are forfeited for desertion, shall be applied, in the first instance, in or towards the reimbursement of the expenses occasioned by such desertion to the master or owner of the ship from which the desertion has taken place; and may, if earned subsequently to the desertion, be recovered by such master, or by the owner or his agent, in the same manner as the deserter might have recovered the same if they had not been forfeited; and in any legal proceeding relating to such wages, the court may order the same to be paid accordingly; and subject to such reimbursement, the same shall be paid to the Minister of Finance and Receiver General, to form part of the Consolidated Revenue Fund of Canada; and in all other cases of forfeiture of wages under the provisions hereinbefore contained, the forfeiture shall, in the absence of of any specific directions to the contrary, be for the benefit of the master or owner by whom the wages are payable. 38 V., c. 29, s. 24.

26. Any question concerning the forfeiture of or deductions from the wages of any seaman, belonging to any ship subject to the provisions of this Act, may be determined in any proceeding in Canada, lawfully instituted with respect to such wages, notwithstanding that the offence in respect of which such question arises, though hereby made punishable by imprisonment as well as forfeiture, has not been made the subject of any criminal proceeding. 38 V., c. 29, s. 25.

Question of forfeiture may be decided in suits for wages.

27. If any seaman, on or before being engaged in any ship subject to the provisions of this Act, wilfully and fraudulently makes a false statement of the name of his last ship or last alleged ship, or wilfully and fraudulently makes a false statement of his own name, he shall incur a penalty not exceeding twenty dollars; and such penalty may be deducted from any wages he earns by virtue of such engagement as aforesaid, and shall, subject to reimbursement of the loss and expenses, if any, occasioned by any previous desertion, be paid and applied in the same manner as other penalties payable under this Act. 38 V., c. 29, s. 26.

Penalty for false statement as to ship or name.

ENTICING TO DESERT AND HARBORING DESERTERS.

28. Every person who, by any means whatsoever, persuades or attempts to persuade any seaman, belonging to any ship subject to the provisions of this Act, to neglect or refuse to join or to desert from his ship, or to absent himself from his duty, shall, for the first offence in respect of each such seaman, be liable to imprisonment, with hard labour, for a term not exceeding six months and not less than one month, and for any subsequent offence, in respect to each such seaman, be liable to imprisonment, with hard labour, for a term not exceeding twelve months and not less than two months; and every person who wilfully harbors or secretes any such seaman who has deserted from his ship, or who has wilfully neglected or refused to join his ship, knowing or having reason to believe such seaman to have so done shall, for every such seaman so harbored or secreted, be liable to imprisonment, with hard labour, for a term not exceeding six months and not less than one month, and for any subsequent offence, for a term not exceeding twelve months and not less than two months. 38 V., c. 29, s. 27.

Punishment for enticing to desert or harboring deserters.

CHANGE OF MASTER.

29. If, during the progress of a voyage, the master of any ship subject to the provisions of this Act is superseded in Canada, or, for any other reason, quits the ship and is succeeded in the

On change of master, certain documents to be

handed over to his successor. command by some other person, he shall deliver to his successor the certificate of registry and the various documents relating to the navigation of the ship and to the crew thereof, which are in his custody, and shall, in default, incur a penalty not exceeding four hundred dollars. 38 V., c. 29, s. 28.

MODE OF RECOVERING WAGES.

Seamen may sue for wages in a summary manner.

30. Any seaman or apprentice belonging to any ship subject to the provisions of this Act, or any person duly authorized on his behalf, may sue in a summary manner before any judge of the Superior Court for Lower Canada, judge of the sessions of the peace, judge of a county court, stipendiary magistrate, police magistrate, or any two justices of the peace acting in or near the place at which the service has terminated, or at which the seaman or apprentice has been discharged, or at which any master or owner or other person upon whom the claim is made is or resides, for any amount of wages due to such seaman or apprentice not exceeding $200 over and above the costs of any proceeding for the recovery thereof, as soon as the same becomes payable; and such judge, magistrate or justices may, upon complaint on oath made to him or them by such seaman or apprentice, or on his behalf, summon such master or owner, or other person to appear before him or them to answer such complaint. 45 V., c. 34, s. 2, *part*;—36 V., c. 129, s. 52.

Summons.

Judges may make order for payment of wages.

31. Upon appearance of such master or owner, or in default thereof, on due proof of his having been so summoned, such judge, magistrate or justices may examine upon the oath of the respective witnesses of the parties, if there are any, or upon the oath of either of the parties, in case one of the parties requires such oath from the other, before such judge, magistrate or justices, touching the complaint and amount of wages due, and may make such order for the payment thereof, as to such judge, magistrate or justices appears reasonable and just; and any order made by such judge, magistrate or justices shall be final. 45 V., c. 34, s. 2, *part*;—36 V., c. 129, s. 53.

Warrant of distress may be issued.

32. If such order is not obeyed within twenty-four hours next after the making thereof, such judge, magistrate or justices may issue a warrant to levy the amount of the wages awarded to be due, by the distress and sale of the goods and chattels of the person on whom such order is made,—paying to such person the overplus of the produce of the sale, after deducting therefrom all the charges and expenses incurred by the seaman or apprentice in the making and hearing of the complaint, as well as those incurred by the distress and levy, and in the enforcement of the order. 45 V., c. 34, s. 2, *part*;—36 V., c. 129, s. 54.

If sufficient distress cannot be found wages and expenses may be levied on ship, or person may be committed.

33. If sufficient distress cannot be found, such judge, magistrate or justices may cause the amount of such wages and expenses to be levied on the ship in respect of the service on board which the wages are claimed, or the tackle and apparel thereof; and if such ship is not within the jurisdiction of such judge, magistrate or justices, they may cause the person on whom the order for payment is made to be apprehended and committed to the common gaol of the locality, or if there is no gaol there, then to that which is nearest to the locality, for a term not exceeding three months, and not less than one month, under each such condemnation. 45 V., c. 34, s. 2, *part*;—36 V., c. 129, s. 55.

34. No suit or proceedings for the recovery of wages under the sum of two hundred dollars shall be instituted by or on behalf of any seaman or apprentice belonging to any ship subject to the provisions of this Act, in any court of Vice-Admiralty, or in the Maritime Court of Ontario, or in any superior court, unless the owner of the ship is insolvent within the meaning of any Act respecting insolvency, for the time being in force in Canada, or unless the ship is under arrest or is sold by the authority of any such court as aforesaid, or unless any judge, magistrate or justices, acting under the authority of this Act, refer the case to be adjudged by such court, or unless neither the owner nor the master is or resides within twenty miles of the place where the seaman or apprentice is discharged or put ashore. 45 V., c. 34, s. 2, *part*;—36 V., c. 129, s. 56. **Restrictions on suits for wages in superior courts.**

35. If any suit for the recovery of a seaman's wages is instituted against any such ship, or the master or owner thereof, in any court of Vice-Admiralty, or in the Maritime Court of Ontario, or in any superior court in Canada, and it appears to the court, in the course of such suit, that the plaintiff might have had as effectual a remedy for the recovery of his wages by complaint to a judge, magistrate or two justices of the peace under this Act, then the judge shall certify to that effect, and thereupon no costs shall be awarded to the plaintiff. 45 V., c. 34, s. 2, *part*;—36 V., c. 129, s. 57. **If suits are brought unnecessarily before superior court, no costs to plaintiff.**

LEGAL PROCEDURE.

36. The time for instituting summary proceedings under this Act shall be limited as follows, that is to say:— **Limitation of time in summary proceedings.**

(*a.*) No conviction for any offence shall be made in any summary proceeding under this Act, unless such proceeding is commenced within six months after the commision of the offence, or—if both or either of the parties to such proceeding happen, during such time, to be out of Canada, or not to be within the jurisdiction of any court capable of dealing with the case—unless the same is commenced within two months after they both first happen to arrive or to be at one time within Canada, or within such jurisdiction; **Summary convictions.**

(*b.*) No order for the payment of money shall be made in any summary proceeding under this Act, unless such proceeding is commenced within six months after the cause of complaint arises, or—if both or either of the parties happen, during such time, to be out of Canada—unless the same is commenced within six months after they both first happen to arrive or to be at one time within Canada. 38 V., c. 29, s. 29. **Orders for payment of money.**

37. Any judge of the Superior Court for Lower Canada, judge of the sessions of the peace, judge of a county court, police magistrate, stipendiary magistrate or any two justices of **How offences shall be dealt with.**

the peace shall have authority and jurisdiction to try and determine in a summary way all offences punishable under this Act, whether by fine, penalty or imprisonment, or by both fine and imprisonment, or penalty and imprisonment.

Act respecting summary proceedings to apply.

38. The provisions of the Act intituled "*An Act respecting summary proceedings before justices of the peace,*" shall apply to and govern proceedings against any person for any offence against this Act, and a judge of the Superior Court, a judge of the sessions of the peace, a judge of a county court, a police magistrate or stipendiary magistrate, before whom any proceedings under this Act are taken, shall, for the purposes of the said proceedings, have all the powers of two justices of the peace.

Recovery of penalties.

Imprisonment if not paid.

39. All penalties imposed by this Act may be recovered, with costs, upon the oath of one credible witness other than the informer, and shall be paid over to the Minister of Finance and Receiver General, to be disposed of as the Governor in Council directs, and in case of non-payment, shall be levied by distress and sale of the offender's goods and chattels, by warrant under the hand and seal of the convicting judge, magistrate or justices of the peace, directed to a constable or other peace officer; and the overplus, if any, after deducting the penalty and costs of suit, together with the expenses of the distress and sale, shall be returned to the owner; and for want of sufficient distress, the offender shall be committed, by warrant under the hand and seal of the judge, magistrate or justices, to the common gaol of the locality, or if there is no common goal there, then to that common gaol which is nearest to that locality, for any term not exceeding six months; and such judge, magistrate or justices shall also award and order the imprisonment, if any, to which the offender is liable for the offence whereby the penalty is incurred. 38 V., c. 29, s. 30.

Evidence of seamen concernd. to be received.

40. In all cases of complaints made by or on behalf of any seaman under this Act, the evidence of such seaman shall be received and taken, notwithstanding that he is interested in the matter 38 V., c. 29, s. 31, *part.*

No appeal; and conviction not to be quashed for want of form or removed by *certiorari*.

41. There shall be no appeal from any conviction or order adjudged or made under this Act, by or before any judge of the Superior Court for Lower Canada, judge of the county court, judge of the sessions of the peace, police magistrate, stipendiary magistrate or any two justices of the peace, for any offence against this Act; and no conviction under this Act shall be quashed for want of form, or be removed by *certiorari* or otherwise into any superior court; and no warrant of commitment under this Act shall be held void by reason of any defect therein, if it is therein alleged that the party has been convicted, and there is a good and valid conviction to sustain the same. 38 V., c. 29, s. 32.

Justices may grant warrant to search for seamen un-

42. Any justice of the peace, at any port or place in Canada, on complaint before him on the oath of one or more credible witness or witnesses, that any seaman under this Act is concealed or secreted in any dwelling house or outhouse, or on board of any ship or elsewhere, shall grant a warrant under his hand and seal, addressed to a constable or constables there, commanding him or them to make diligent and immediate search, in or about such dwelling house or out-house, or on board such ship, or such other place or places as are specified in the warrant, and to bring before him every such seaman found concealed, whether named in the warrant or not. 38 V., c. 29, s. 33.

lawfully harbored or secreted.

Police officers or constables to assist in enforcing this Act.

43. Any police officer or constable required under the provisions of this Act to give assistance to the master or any mate, or the owner, ship's husband or consignee of any ship in apprehending, with or without a warrant, any seaman duly engaged to serve in such ship, and neglecting or refusing to proceed to sea therein, or being found otherwise absenting himself therefrom without leave, may, at any time, enter into any tavern, inn, ale house, beer house, seamen's boarding house, or other house or place of entertainment, or into any shop or other place wherein liquors or refreshments are sold or reputed to be sold, whether legally or illegally, or into any house of ill fame; and any person being therein, or having charge thereof, who refuses, or after due demand fails to admit such police officer or constable into the same, or offers any obstruction to his admission thereto, shall, for every such offence, incur a penalty not exceeding fifty dollars and not less than ten dollars. 38 V., c. 29, s. 34.

Penalty for obstructing search, etc.

SCHE

AGREEMENT, or Articles, for a

Name of Ship.	Official Number.	Port of Registry.	Port No. and Date of Register.	Registered Tonnage.	MANAGING
					Name.

The several persons whose names are hereto subscribed, and whose descriptions are contained the several capacities expressed against their respective names, on a voyage from *a*

And the said Crew agree to conduct themselves in an orderly, faithful, honest and sober manner, and to be obedient to the lawful commands of the said Master, or of any person who shall lawfully relating to the said Ship, and the stores and cargo thereof, whether on board, in boats, or on shore; the said Master hereby agrees to pay to the said Crew as wages the sums against their names respect according to the usual custom: And it is hereby agreed that any embezzlement or wilful or negligent be made good to the owner out of the wages of the person guilty of the same: And if any person enters to perform, his wages shall be reduced in proportion to his incompetency: And it is also agreed that *c*

In witness whereof the said parties have subscribed their names hereto on the days against

Signed by__________________________Master, on the__________

Signatures of Crew.	Age.	Where Born.	Ship in which he last served, Official Number, and Port she belonged to, or other Employment.	Date and place of Discharge from such Ship.	
				Date.	Place.

PLACE OF SIGNATURES AND

NOTE.—Here the entries

NOTE.—Any Erasure, Interlineation or Alteration in this Agreement, except in the case of Substitutes, will be void, unless attested by some Shipping Master, Officer of Customs, Consul, or Vice-Consul, or other respectable witnesses to be made with the consent of the persons interested.

DULE.

Canadian Ship, subject to this Act.

OWNER.	MASTER.			Date and Place of first Signature of Agreement, including Name of Shipping Office.
Address.	Name.	No. of Certificate.	Address.	

below, hereby agree to serve on board the said Ship, in (*or*, which Ship is to be employed[b])

and to be at all times diligent in their respective duties, succeed him, and of their superior officers, in everything in consideration of which services to be duly performed, ively expressed, and to supply them with provisions destruction of any part of the Ship's cargo or stores shall himself as qualified for a duty which he proves incompetent

[a] Here the voyage is to be described, and the places named at which the Ship is to touch, or if that cannot be done, the general nature and probable length of the voyage is to be stated.

[b] Here state probable nature of Ship's employment, or nature of voyage and period of engagement.

[c] Here any other stipulations may be inserted to which the parties may agree, and which are not contrary to law.

their respective signatures mentioned.

day of__________18__.

Date and Place of joining this Ship.		In what capacity engaged; and if Mate, No. of his certificate (if any).	Time at which he is to be on board.	Amount of Wages per Calendar Month, Share, or Voyage.		Shipping Master's or Witness' Signature.
Date.	Place.			$	cts.	

DESCRIPTIONS OF SUBSTITUTES.

are to be made as above.

I declare to the truth of the entries in this Agreement.

________________*Master.*

INDORSEMENTS.	INDORSEMENTS.	INDORSEMENTS.

NAVIGATION OF CANADIAN WATERS.

Revised Statutes of Canada, Chapter 79.

A.D. 1886.

An Act respecting the Navigation of Canadian Waters.

HER Majesty, by and with the advice and consent of the Senate and House of Commons of Canada, enacts as follows:

INTERPRETATION.

Interpretation.

1. In this Act, unless the context otherwise requires,—

"Vessel."

(*a.*) The expression "vessel" includes every description of vessel used in navigation;

"Ship."

(*b.*) The expression "ship" includes every description of vessel not propelled by oars;

"Steamboat" or "steamship."

(*c.*) The expression "steamship" or "steamboat" includes every vessel propelled wholly or in part by steam or by any machinery or power other than sails or oars;

"Practice of "seamen."

(*d.*) The expression "ordinary practice of seamen," as applied to any case, means and includes the ordinary practice of skilful and careful persons engaged in navigating the waters of Canada in like cases;

"Owner."

(*e.*) The expression "owner" includes the lessee or charterer of any vessel having the control of the navigation thereof. 43 V., c. 29, s. 3.

REGULATIONS FOR PREVENTING COLLISIONS.

Extent of application of the following rules.

2. The following rules with respect to lights, fog signals, steering and sailing and rafts, shall apply to all the rivers, lakes and other navigable waters within Canada, or within the jurisdiction of the Parliament thereof; that is to say:—

Preliminary.

Steam-ships under sail or under steam.

Art. 1. In the following rules every steamship which is under sail, and not under steam, is to be considered a sailing ship; and every steamship which is under steam, whether under sail or not, is to be considered a ship under steam.

Rules concerning Lights.

What lights shall be carried.

Art. 2. The lights mentioned in the following Articles, numbered 3, 4, 5, 6, 7, 8, 9, 10 and 11, and no others, shall be carried in all weathers, from sunset to sunrise.

By steamships under way.

Art. 3. A steamship when under way shall carry—

(*a.*) On or in front of the foremast, at a height above the hull of not less than twenty feet, and if the breadth of the ship exceeds twenty feet, then at a height above the hull not less than such breadth, a bright white light, so constructed as to show an uniform and unbroken light over an arc of the horizon of twenty points of the compass,—so fixed as to throw the light ten points on each side of the ship, viz., from right ahead to two points abaft the beam on either side,—and of such a character as to be visible on a dark night, with a clear atmosphere, at a distance of at least five miles; **At foremast head.**

(*b.*) On the starboard side, a green light so constructed as to show an uniform and unbroken light over an arc of the horizon of ten points of the compass,—so fixed as to throw the light from right ahead to two points abaft the beam on the starboard side,—and of such a character as to be visible on a dark night, with a clear atmosphere, at a distance of at least two miles; **On starboard side.**

(*c.*) On the port side, a red light, so constructed as to show an uniform and unbroken light over an arc of the horizon of ten points of the compass,—so fixed as to throw the light from right ahead to two points abaft the beam on the port side,—and of such a character as to be visible on a dark night, with a clear atmosphere, at a distance of at least two miles; **On port side.**

(*d.*) The said green and red side lights shall be fitted with in-board screens projecting at least three feet forward from the light, so as to prevent these lights from being seen across the bow. **How to be fitted.**

Art. 4. A steamship, when towing another ship, a raft or rafts, shall, in addition to her side lights, carry two bright white lights in a vertical line, one over the other, not less than three feet apart, so as to distinguish her from other steamships: each of these lights shall be of the same construction and character, and shall be carried in the same position as the white light which other steamships are required to carry. **By steam-ships towing.**

Art. 5. A ship, whether a steamship or a sailing ship, when employed either in laying or in picking up a telegraph cable, or which from any accident is not under command, shall at night carry, in the same position as the white light which steamships are required to carry, and, if a steamship, in place of that light, three red lights in globular lanterns, each not less than ten inches in diameter, in a vertical line one over the other, not less than three feet apart: and shall by day carry in a vertical line one over the other, not less than three feet apart, in front of but not lower than her foremost head, three black balls or shapes, each two feet in diameter; **Lights and shapes, by steam or sailing ships when not under command.**

(*a.*) These shapes and lights are to be taken by approaching ships as signals that the ship using them is not under command, and cannot therefore get out of the way; **What to denote.**

(*b.*) The above ships, when not making any way through the water, shall not carry the side lights, but when making way shall carry them. **When to carry side lights.**

Art. 6. A sailing ship under way, or being towed, shall carry the same lights as are provided by Article 3 for a steamship under way, with the exception of the white light,—which she shall never carry. **By sailing ships in motion.**

Art. 7. Whenever, as in the case of small vessels during bad weather, the green and red side lights cannot be fixed, these lights shall be kept on deck, on their respective sides of the vessel, ready **By small vessels in bad weather.**

for use; and shall, on the approach of or to other vessels, be exhibited on their respective sides in sufficient time to prevent collision, in such manner as to make them most visible, and so that the green light shall not be seen on the port side nor the red light on the starboard side:

Lanterns to be painted outside. To make the use of these portable lights more certain and easy, the lanterns containing them shall each be painted outside with the colour of the light they respectively contain, and shall be provided with proper screens.

By ships at anchor. Art. 8. A ship, whether a steamship or a sailing ship, when at anchor, shall carry, where it can best be seen, but at a height not exceeding twenty feet above the hull, a white light in a globular lantern of not less than eight inches in diameter, and so constructed as to show a clear, uniform and unbroken light visible all around the horizon, and at a distance of at least one mile.

By pilot vessels on duty. Art. 9. A pilot vessel, when engaged on her station on pilotage duty, shall not carry the lights required for other vessels, but shall carry a white light at the masthead, visible all around the horizon, and shall also exhibit a flare-up light or flare-up lights at short intervals, which shall never exceed fifteen minutes:

When not on duty. (*a.*) A pilot vessel, when not engaged on her station on pilotage duty, shall carry lights similar to those of other ships.

Open fishing and other boats. Art. 10. (*a.*) Open fishing boats and other open boats when under way shall not be obliged to carry the side lights required for other vessels; but every such boat shall, in lieu thereof, have ready at hand a lantern with a green glass on the one side and a red glass on the other side; and on the approach of or to other vessels, such lantern shall be exhibited in sufficient time to prevent collision, so that the green light shall not be seen on the port side, nor the red light on the starboard side;

When at anchor. (*b.*) A fishing vessel, and an open boat, when at the anchor, shall exhibit a bright white light;

Fishing vessels when drift net fishing. (*c.*) A fishing vessel, when employed in drift net fishing, shall carry on one of her masts two red lights in a vertical line one over the other, not less than three feet apart;

Trawlers at work. (*d.*) A trawler at work shall carry on one of her masts two lights in a vertical line one over the other, not less than three feet apart, the upper light red, and the lower green, and shall also either carry the side lights required for other vessels, or, if the side lights cannot be carried, have ready at hand the colored lights as provided in Article 7, or a lantern with a red and a green glass as described in paragraph (*a*) of this Article;

Flare-up lights. (*e.*) Fishing vessels and open boats shall not be prevented from using a flare-up light in addition, if they desire so to do;

The said lights substituted for those under convention with France. (*f.*) The lights mentioned in this article are substituted for those mentioned in the 12th, 13th and 14th Articles of the Convention between France and England scheduled to the "*British Sea Fisheries Act*, 1868;"

Lanterns for lights. (*g.*) All lights required by this Article, except side lights, shall be in globular lanterns, so constructed as to show all round the horizon.

Ship overtaken by another. Art. 11. A ship which is being overtaken by another shall show from her stern to such last-mentioned ship a white light or a flare-up light.

Sound Signals for Fog, &c.

Art. 12. A steam-ship shall be provided with a steam whistle or other efficient steam sound signal, so placed that the sound may not be intercepted by any obstruction, and also with an efficient bell. A sailing-ship shall be provided with an efficient fog horn, to be sounded by a bellows or other mechanical means, and also with an efficient bell: **Steam-ships to have certain sound signals.**

In fog, mist, or falling snow, whether by day or night, the signals described in this Article shall be used as follows; that is to say:— **In fogs, &c.**

(*a.*) A steam-ship under way shall make with her steam whistle or other steam sound signal, at intervals of not more than two minutes, a prolonged blast; **Blasts at intervals by steam-ships.**

(*b.*) A sailing-ship under way shall make with her fog horn, at intervals of not more than two minutes, when on the starboard tack one blast, when on the port tack two blasts in succession, and when with the wind abaft the beam, three blasts in succession; **Signals by fog horn by sailing-ships.**

(*c.*) A steam-ship and a sailing-ship, when not under way shall, at intervals of not more than two minutes, ring the bell. **By ringing bell.**

Speed of Ships to be moderate in Fog, &c.

Art. 13. Every ship, whether a sailing-ship or steam-ship shall, in a fog, mist, or falling snow, go at a moderate speed. **Speed restricted in fog, &c.**

Steering and Sailing Rules.

Art. 14. When two sailing-ships are approaching one another, so as to involve risk of collision, one of them shall keep out of the way of the other, as follows, that is to say:— **Sailing-ships meeting.**

(*a.*) A ship which is running free shall keep out of the way of a ship which is close-hauled;

(*b.*) A ship which is close-hauled on the port tack shall keep out of the way of a ship which is close-hauled on the star-board tack;

(*c.*) When both are running free with the wind on different sides, the ship which has the wind on the port side shall keep out of the way of the other;

(*d.*) When both are running free with the wind on the same side, the ship which is to windward shall keep out of the way of the ship which is to leeward;

(*e.*) A ship which has the wind aft shall keep out of the way of the other ship.

Art. 15. If two ships under steam are meeting end on, or nearly end on, so as to involve risk of collision, each shall alter her course to starboard, so that each may pass on the port side of the other: **Steam-ships meeting.**

(*a.*) This Article only applies to cases where ships are meeting end on, or nearly end on, in such a manner as to involve risk of collision, and does not apply to two ships which must, if both keep on their respective courses, pass clear of each other; **Limitation of this article.**

(*b.*) The only cases to which it does apply are, when each of the two ships is end on, or nearly end on, to the other; in other words, to cases in which, by day, each ship sees the masts of the other in **Cases to which it applies.**

a line, or nearly in a line with her own; and by night, to cases in which each ship is in such a position as to see both the side lights of the other;

Cases to which it does not apply. (*c.*) It does not apply by day, to cases in which a ship sees another ahead crossing her own course, or by night, to cases where the red light of one ship is opposed to the red light of the other, or where the green light of one ship is opposed to the green light of the other, or where a red light without a green light, or a green light without a red light, is seen ahead, or where both green and red lights are seen anywhere but ahead.

Steam-ships crossing. Art. 16. If two ships under steam are crossing, so as to involve risk of collision, the ship which has the other on her own starboard side shall keep out of the way of the other.

Steam-ships and sailing ships. Art. 17. If two ships, one of which is a sailing-ship and the other a steam-ship, are proceeding in such directions as to involve risk of collision, the steam-ship shall keep out of the way of the sailing ship.

Steam-ships nearing a vessel. Art. 18. Every steam-ship when approaching another ship, so as to involve risk of collision, shall slacken her speed or stop and reverse, if necessary.

How steam-ships may signal by steam. Art. 19. In taking any course authorized or required by these regulations, a steam-ship under way may indicate that course to any other ship which she has in sight by the following signals on her steam whistle, that is to say:—

One short blast to mean "I am directing my course to starboard";

Two short blasts to mean "I am directing my course to port";

Three short blasts to mean "I am going full speed astern:"

Signalling to be optional. The use of these signals is optional; but if they are used, the course of the ship must be in accordance with the signal made.

Ship overtaking another. Art. 20. Notwithstanding anything contained in any preceeding Article, every ship, whether a sailing-ship or a steam-ship, overtaking any other, shall keep out of the way of the overtaken ship.

Steam-ships in narrow channels. Art. 21. In narrow channels every steam-ship shall, when it is safe and practicable, keep to that side of the fairway or mid-channel which lies on the starboard side of such ship.

Ship keeping out of the way Art. 22. When by the above rules one of two ships is to keep out of the way, the other shall keep her course.

Regard to be had to dangers of navigation. Art. 23. In obeying and construing these rules, due regard shall be had to all dangers of navigation, and to any special circumstances which may render a departure from the above rules necessary in order to avoid immediate danger.

No ship, under any circumstances, to neglect proper precautions.

Rules not to excuse. Art. 24. Nothing in these rules shall exonerate any ship, or the owner or master or crew thereof, from the consequences of any neglect to carry lights or signals, or of any neglect to keep a proper look-out, or of the neglect of any precaution required by the ordinary practice of seamen, or by the special circumstances of the case.

Reservation of Rules for Harbors and Island Navigation.

Rules by local authorities. Art. 25. Nothing in these rules shall interfere with the operation of a special rule, duly made by local authority, relative to the navigation of any harbor, river or inland navigation.

Special Lights for Squadrons and Convoys.

Art. 26. Nothing in these rules shall interfere with the operation of any special rules made by the Government of any nation with respect to additional station and signal lights for two or more ships of war or for ships sailing under convoy. **Squadrons or convoys.**

Rafts and Harbor of Sorel.

Art. 27. Rafts, while drifting or at anchor on any of the waters of Canada, shall have a bright fire kept burning on them from sunset to sunrise. Whenever any raft is going in the same direction as another which is ahead, the one shall be so navigated as not to come within twenty yards of the other, and every vessel meeting or overtaking a raft shall keep out of the way thereof. Rafts shall be so navigated and anchored as not to cause any unnecessary impediment or obstruction to vessels navigating the same waters. **Rules for rafts.** **Not to obstruct vessels.**

Art. 28. Unless it is otherwise directed by the Harbor Commissioners of Montreal, ships and vessels entering or leaving the harbor of Sorel shall take the port side, anything in the preceding articles to the contrary notwithstanding. **Harbor of Sorel.**

Art. 29. The rules of navigation contained in Articles 27 and 28, shall be subject to the provisions contained in Articles 23 and 24. 43 V., c. 29, s. 2;—44 V., c. 21, s. 2;—49 V., c. 4, s. 2 *and* schedule. **As to articles 27 and 28.**

LOCAL BY-LAWS, PENALTIES, ETC.

3. No rule or by-law of the Harbour Commissioners of Montreal or the Trinity House of Quebec, or Quebec Harbour Commissioners, or other local rule or by-law inconsistent with this Act, shall be of any force or effect; but so far as it is not inconsistent with this Act. any such rule or by-law made by the said Harbour Commissioners of Montreal or Trinity House of Quebec, or Quebec Harbour Commissioners, or other competent local authority, shall be of full force and effect within the locality to which it applies. 43 V., c. 29, s. 4. **Provisions as to local by-laws and rules.**

4. All owners, masters and persons in charge of any ship, vessel, or raft, shall obey the rules prescribed by this Act, and shall not carry and exhibit any other lights or use any other fog signals than such as are required by the said rules; and in case of wilful default, such master or person in charge, or such owner, if it appears that he was in fault, shall, for each occasion on which any of the said rules is violated, incur a penalty not exceeding two hundred dollars and not less than twenty dollars. 43 V., c. 29, s. 5. **Penalty for wilful disobedience of this Act.**

5. If, in any case of collision, it appears to the court before which the case is tried, that such collision was occasioned by the non-observance of any of the rules prescribed by this Act, the vessel or raft by which such rules have been violated shall be deemed to be in fault; unless it can be shown to the satisfaction of the court that the circumstances of the case rendered a departure from the said rules necessary. 43 V., c. 29, s. 6. **Collision from non-observance of rules.**

Liability for damage occasioned by non-observance of rules.

6. If any damage to person or property arises from the non-observance by any vessel or raft of any of the rules prescribed by this Act, such damage shall be deemed to have been occasioned by the wilful default of the person in charge of such raft, or of the deck of such vessel at the time, unless the contrary is proved, or it is shown to the satisfaction of the court that the circumstances of the case rendered a departure from the said rules necessary; and the owner of the vessel or raft, in all civil proceedings, and the master or person in charge as aforesaid, or the owner,—if it appears that he was in fault,—in all proceedings, civil or criminal, shall be subject to the legal consequences of such default. 43 V., c. 29, s. 7.

Case where both vessels are in fault.

Imp. Act 36 37 V., c. 66.

7. In any cause or proceeding for damages arising out of a collision between two vessels, or a vessel and a raft, if both vessels or both the vessel and the raft are found to have been in fault, the rules heretofore in force in the Court of Admiralty in England, and now in Her Majesty's High Court of Justice, under the "*Supreme Court of Judicature Act*, 1873," so far as they are at variance with the rules in force in the courts of common law, shall prevail, and the damages shall be borne equally by the two vessels, or the vessel and the raft, one-half by each. 43 V., c. 29, s. 8.

Recovery of penalties.

If not paid.

Application.

Exception.

8. Unless herein otherwise provided, all penalties incurred under this Act may be recovered in the name of Her Majesty, by any inspector of steam-boats, or by any person aggrieved by any act, neglect or wilful omission by which the penalty is incurred, before any two justices of the peace, on the evidence of one credible witness; and in default of payment of such penalty, such justices may commit the offender to gaol for any term not exceeding three months; and, except as hereinafter provided, all penalties recovered under this Act shall be paid over to the Minister of Finance and Receiver General, and shall be by him placed at the credit of and shall form part of the Steam-boat Inspection Fund: Provided always, that all penalties incurred for any offence against this Act shall, if such offence is committed within the jurisdiction of the Quebec Harbour Commissioners, or of the Harbour Commissioners of Montreal, be sued for, recovered, enforced and applied in like manner as penalties imposed for the violation of the by-laws of the said Harbour Commissioners within whose jurisdiction the offence is committed. 43 V., c. 29, s. 9.

Foreign ships in Canadian waters.

9. Whenever foreign ships are within Canadian waters, the rules for preventing collisions prescribed by this Act, and all provisions of this Act relating to such rules, or otherwise relating to collisions, shall apply to such foreign ships; and in any case arising in any court of justice in Canada concerning matters happening within Canadian waters, foreign ships shall, so far as regards such rules and provisions, be treated as if they were British or Canadian ships. 43 V., c. 29, s. 11.

DUTY OF MASTERS; LIABILITY OF OWNERS OF SHIPS.

Duties of masters of vessels

10. In every case of collision between two ships, the person in charge of each ship shall, if and so far as he can do so without danger to his own ship and crew, render to the other ship, her master, crew and passengers, such assistance as is practicable, and as is necessary in order to save them from any danger caused by such collision; and shall also give to the master or other person in charge of the other ship the name of his own ship and of her port of registry, or of the port or place to which she belongs, and also the names of the ports and places from which and to which she is bound; and if he fails so to do, and no reasonable excuse for such failure is shown, the collision shall, in the absence of proof to the contrary, be deemed to have been caused by his wrongful act, neglect or default. 43 V., c. 29, s. 12, *part.* In case of collision. Penalty for default.

11. Every master or person in charge of a British or Canadian ship, who fails, without reasonable cause, to render such assistance, or to give such information as aforesaid, is guilty of a misdemeanor; and if he is a certificated officer under Canadian authority, an inquiry into his conduct may be held, and his certificate may be cancelled or suspended. 43 V., c. 29, s. 12, *part.* Further penalty in case of British or Canadian ships.

12. The owners of any ship, whether British, Canadian or foreign, shall not, whenever all or any of the following events occur without their actual fault or privity, that is to say:— Liability of owners limited in case of collision without their fault.

(*a.*) When any loss of life or personal injury is caused to any person being carried in such ship;

(*b.*) When any damage or loss is caused to any goods, merchandise or other things whatsoever on board any such ship;

(*c.*) When any loss of life or personal injury is, by reason of the improper navigation of such ship as aforesaid, caused to any person in any ship or boat;

(*d.*) When any loss or damage is, by reason of the improper navigation of such ship as aforesaid, caused to any other ship or boat, or to any goods or merchandise or to other things whatsoever on board any other ship or boat,—

Be answerable in damages in respect of loss of life or personal injury, either alone or together with loss or damage to ships, boats, goods, merchandise or other things, nor in respect of loss or damage to ships, goods, merchandise or other things, whether there is in addition loss of life or personal injury or not, to an aggregate amount exceeding thirty-eight dollars and ninety-two cents for each ton of the ship's tonnage,—such tonnage to be the registered tonnage in the case of sailing-ships; and in the case of steam-ships the gross tonnage without deduction on account of engine-room; Extreme amount recoverable. Tonnage.

2. In the case of any British or Canadian ship, such tonnage shall be the registered or gross tonnage, according to the British or Canadian law, and in the case of a foreign ship which has been or can be measured according to British or Canadian law, the tonnage as ascertained by such measurement shall, for the purposes of this section, be deemed to be the tonnage of such ship; How calculated.

3. In the case of any foreign ship which has not been and cannot be measured according to British or Canadian law, the deputy of the Minister of Marine shall, on receiving from or by direction of the court hearing the case, such evidence concerning the dimensions of the ship as it is found practicable to furnish, give a certificate under his hand, stating what would, in his opinion, Tonnage how calculated in certain cases.

have been the tonnage of such ship if she had been duly measured according to Canadian law, and the tonnage so stated in such certificate shall, for the purposes of this section, be deemed to be the tonnage of such ship. 43 V., c. 29, s. 13.

As to insurances in such cases.

13. Insurances effected against any or all of the events enumerated in the section next preceding, and occurring without such actual fault or privity as therein mentioned, shall not be invalid by reason of the nature of the risk. 43 V., c. 29, s. 13.

Provision in case of alteration of Imperial regulations.

14. If Her Majesty, acting on the joint recommendation of the Admiralty and the Board of Trade, by Order in Council annuls or modifies any of the regulations for preventing collisions on navigable waters, which, by Order of Her Majesty in Council of the fourteenth day of August, 1879, were substituted for those theretofore in force for like purposes in the United Kingdom, or make new regulations in addition thereto or in substitution therefor, the Governor in Council may, from time to time, make corresponding changes, as respects Canadian waters, in the regulations contained in the second section of this Act or any that may be substituted for them,—or may suspend them or any of them, and make others in their stead,—or may revive all or any of the regulations in the Act of the Parliament of Canada passed in the thirty-first year of Her Majesty's reign, and intituled "*An Act respecting the Navigation of Canadian Waters,*" as he deems best for insuring the correspondence of the regulations of Her Majesty in Council with those of the Governor in Council. 44 V., c. 20, s. 2.

LIST OF OFFICERS

OF THE

MARITIME COURT OF ONTARIO.

JUDGE AND SURROGATES.

Joseph Easton Macdougall	Judge,	Toronto.
Charles John Robinson	Surrogate,	Sarnia.
Edmund John Senkler	"	St. Catharines.
Henry Macpherson	"	Owen Sound.
Isaac Francis Toms		Goderich.
Jacob Farrand Pringle		Cornwall.
Cornelius Vallean Price		Kingston.
William Henry Ritchey Allison	"	Picton.
John Juchereau Kingsmill		Walkerton.
James S. Sinclair		Hamilton.
John Anderson Ardagh		Collingwood.
Charles Robert Horne		Sandwich.
Robert Thompson Livingstone		Simcoe.
Robert Stuart Woods	"	Chatham.
Walter McCrea		Sault St. Marie.
John Macpherson Hamilton		Port Arthur.

REGISTRAR AND DEPUTY REGISTRARS.

John Bruce	Registrar,	Toronto.
James Alexander Henderson	Deputy Registrar,	Kingston.
Frederick William Macdonald	"	St. Catharines.
Clarence Campbell Rapelje	"	Simcoe.
Samuel Smith Macdonell	"	Windsor.
Cornelius David Morden	"	Picton.
Alfred McDonald Knight		Collingwood.
Augustus George Boswell		Cobourg.
Edwy Allan Morden	"	Picton.
William McLean		Walkerton.
Peter Nicholson		Port Arthur.
George Inglis		Owen Sound.
Thomas A. P. Towers		Sault St. Marie.
William James Barber		Sarnia.
Sutherland Malcolmson	"	Goderich.
Alfred T. Light	"	Cornwall.

MARSHAL AND DEPUTY MARSHALS.

William Boyd	Marshal,	Toronto.
Edmund Deedes	Deputy Marshal,	Simcoe.
James Flintoft, Jr.	"	Sarnia.
Joseph Maughan	"	Owen Sound.
Joseph A. Woodruff	"	St. Catharines.
William Ferguson	"	Kingston.
John Alderman Hyde Campbell	"	Windsor.
Patrick Doherty	"	Collingwood.
Augustus Finlay McCuaig	"	Picton.
Orvin Dean	"	Cobourg.
William Sutton	"	Walkerton.
Robert Edgar	"	Owen Sound.
Joseph Wilson	"	Sault St. Marie.
Thomas B. Van Every	"	Goderich.

OFFICIAL REPORTER.

Alexander Downey	Toronto.

LIST OF REPORTED CASES

Decided under "THE MARITIME JURISDICTION ACT, 1877, (ONTARIO)" by the Judge or Surrogate Judges; with certain cases decided ... OF ... of

S.

ige

me

ra

89

ge

ic-

15

o-

S.

on

r-

de

ed

id

s.

h.

f

y

n

MARSHAL AND DEPUTY MARSHALS.

WILLIAM BOYD	Marshal,	Toronto.
EDMUND DEEDES	Deputy Marshal,	Simcoe.
JAMES FLINTOFT, JR..................	"	Sarnia.

Jo
Jo
W
Jo
Pa
A
Of
W
Rc
Jo
Te

AL

NOTICE is hereby given that the following list of persons of nautical or engineering skill or experience to act as assessors in the Maritime Court of Ontario, has been framed by the Judge under the 10th Section of "The Maritime Jurisdiction Act, 1877," and submitted for the approval of the Minister of Justice, and that such list has been approved by the Minister of Justice, namely :—

Captain Robert D. Stupart, R.N., of the City of Toronto.
" Archibald Taylor, " "
" Alexander Stanley, " "
" John Bengough,
" John T. Douglas,
" William Flett,
" James Dick,
" John Kemp,
" Benjamin Tripp,
" George H. Wyatt, "
" William Hall,
" Duncan Sinclair, " "
" John B. Symes, of the Town of Sarnia.
Engineer George Corbett, of the Town of Owen Sound.
" John Hammond " Windsor.
" J. F. Taylor, of the City of St. Catharines.
" Walter J. Meneilly, " Toronto.
" Neil Currie, " "
" Joseph Taylor, " Kingston.
" Hugh Fairgrieve, " Hamilton.
" Thomas Pettigrew, of the Town of Sarnia.
" William Walsh, of the City of St. Catharines.
" John Venables, " Toronto.
" John Neil, " "
" Donald C. Ridout, " "
" John Fensom,

Dated the 18th day of July, A.D. 1878.

Z. A. LASH,
Deputy of the Minister of Justice, Canada.

K. MACKENZIE, *Judge.*
JOHN BRUCE, *Registrar.*
WM. BOYD, *Marshal.*

LIST OF REPORTED CASES

Decided under "THE MARITIME JURISDICTION ACT, 1877, (ONTARIO)" by the Judge or Surrogate Judges; with certain cases decided by the SUPREME COURT OF CANADA, arising under the Act, or from other Provinces upon questions of Maritime Law.

NOTE,—*The Upper Canada Law Journal N. S. is cited by the letters:—L. J. The Canadian Law Times, by:—L. T.*

INDEX TO FORMS.

APPENDIX OF FORMS.

GENERAL INDEX.

[NOTE.—*The General Rules are indexed by reference to the section as well as the page.*]

APPENDIX.

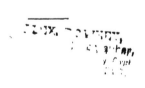

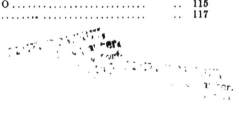

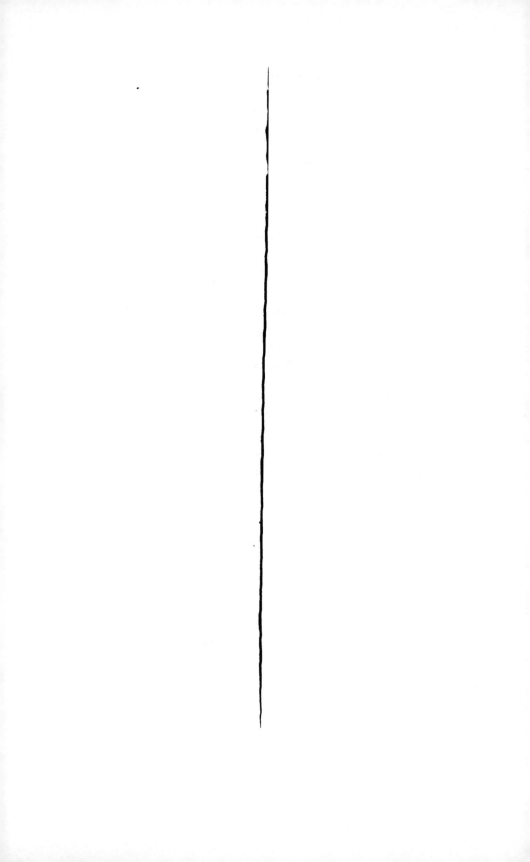

nd

ed,

of

lare

is
ed
the
ose

n,
d
rt
r

ie
alty
ing

ke

ent
d in

ead

xpressions respecti...
... courts ... the judge thereof, ... al
Admiralty shall have jurisdiction accordingly.

AUTHENTICATION OF RECORDS IN U.S. COURTS.

FIRST. By the attest ation of the clerk of such Court, with the seal of such Court annexed, or of the officer in whose custody such records are legally kept, with the seal of his office annexed:

SECOND. By a certificate of the Chief Justice or presiding Magistrate of such Court, that the person attesting such record is the Clerk of the Court, or that he is the officer in whose custody such record is requi by law to be kept; and in either case that the signature such party is genuine; and,

THIRD. By the certificate of the officer of the Government under whose authority such Court is held, ha the custody of the great or principal seal of such Government, purporting that such Court is duly constitu specifying generally the nature of its jurisdiction, verifying the seal of the Court, or of the officer having the custody of such record, and the signature of Chief Justice or presiding Magistrate.

Colonial Courts of Admiralty Act, 1890.

CHAPTER 27.

...t to amend the Law respecting the Exercise of ...miralty Jurisdiction in her Majesty's Dominions and ...sewhere out of the United Kingdom.

(25th July 1890).

...enacted by the Queen's most Excellent Majesty, by and ... the advice and consent of the Lords Spiritual and ...ral, and Commons, in this present Parliament assembled, ...y the authority of the same, as follows:

...t . 1. This Act may be cited as the Colonial Courts of Admiralty Act, 1890.

...ial ...s of ...alty. 2.-(1) Every Court of law in a British possession, which is for the time being declared in pursuance of this Act to be a Court of Admiralty, or which, if no such declaration is ...rce in the possession, has therein original unlimited jurisdiction, shall be a Court of Admiralty, with the ...diction in this Act mentioned, and may for the purpose ...at jurisdiction exercise all the powers which it ...sses for the purpose of its other civil jurisdiction, ...uch court in reference to the jurisdiction conferred ...is Act is in this Act referred to as a Colonial Court ...miralty. ...here in a British possession the Governor ...e sole judicial authority, the expression "court of ... for the purposes of this section includes such ...nor.

...The jurisdiction of a Colonial Court of Admiralty ... subject to the provisions of this Act, be over the ...laces, persons, matters, and things, as the Admiralty ...liction of the High Court in England, whether existing ...tue of any Statute or otherwise, and the Colonial ... of Admiralty may exercise such jurisdiction in like ... and to the same extent as the High Court in ...d, and shall have the same regard as that Court to ...ational law and the comity of nations.

... Subject to the provisions of this Act any enactment ...ing to a Vice-Admiralty Court, which is contained in ... of the Imperial Parliament or in a Colonial law, ... apply to a Colonial Court of Admiralty, and be read ... the expression "Colonial Court of Admiralty" were ... substituted for "Vice-Admiralty Court" or for ... expressions respectively referring to such Vice-...lty Courts or the judges thereof, and the Colonial ...of Admiralty shall have jurisdiction accordingly.

any enactment in an Act of the Imperial Parliament ...ring to the Admiralty Jurisdiction of the High Court in ...and, when applied to a Colonial Court of Admiralty in a ...sh possession, shall be read as if the name of that ...ession were therein substituted for England and Wales;

28 Vict. (b) A Colonial Court of Admiralty shall have under the Naval Prize Act, 1864, and under the
37 Vict. Slave Trade Act, 1873, and any enactment
c. relating to prize or the slave trade, the jurisdiction thereby conferred on a Vice-Admiralty Court and not the jurisdiction

...reby conferred exclusively on the High Court of Admiralt... the High Court of Justice; but unless for the time being ...y authorised, shall not by virtue of this Act exercise ... jurisdiction under the Naval Prize Act, 1864, or ...erwise in relation to prize; and

A Colonial Court of Admiralty shall not have jurisdic...on under this [redacted] Act to try or punish a person for an ...fence which according to the law of England is punishable ... indictment; and

) A Colonial Court of Admiralty shall not have any ...eater jurisdiction in relation to the laws and regulation ...lating to Her Majesty's Navy at sea, or under any Act ...oviding for the discipline of Her Majesty's Navy, than ...y be from time to time conferred on such court by Order ...n Council.

(4) Where a Court in a British possession exercises in ...espect of matters arising outside the body of a country or ...ther like part of a British possession any jurisdiction ...xercisable under this Act, that jurisdiction shall be ...eemed to be exercised under this Act and not otherwise.

3. The legislature of a British possession may by any Colonial law

Power of Colonial legislature as to Admiralty jurisdiction.

(a) declare any Court of unlimited civil jurisdiction, whether original or appelate, in that possession to be a Colonial Court of Admiralty, and provide for the exercise by such Court of its jurisdiction under this Act, and limit territorially, or otherwise, the extent o... such jurisdiction; and

(b) confer upon any inferior or subordinate court in that possession such partial or limited Admiralty jurisdiction under such regulations and with such appeal (if any) as may seem fit:

Provided that any such Colonial law shall not confer any jurisdiction which is not by this Act conferred upon a Colonial Court of Admiralty.

ing e

and,

cessi

28

37

aret

the

j

ter

on

en

in

ea

ua

ov

ns

ch

xe

a) Any enactment in an Act of the Imperial Parliament eferring to the Admiralty Jurisdiction of the High Court i ngland, when applied to a Colonial Court of Admiralty in a ritish possession, shall be read as if the name of that ossession were therein substituted for England and ales; nd

7 & 28 Vict. c.25 — (b) A Colonial Court of Admiralty shall have under the Naval Prize Act, 1864, and under th

6 & 37 Vict. c.88. — Slave Trade Act, 1873, and any enactment relating to prize or the slave trade, the jurisdiction thereby conferred on a Vice-Admiralty Court and not the jurisdiction thereby conferred exclusively on the High Court of Admiralt or the High Court of Justice; but unless for the time being duly authorised, shall not by virtue of this Act exercise any jurisdiction under the Naval Prize Act , 1864, or otherwise in relation to prize; and

(c) A Colonial Court of Admiralty shall not have jurisdiction under this [redacted] Act to try or punish a person for an offence which according to the law of England is punishable on indictment; and

(d) A Colonial Court of Admiralty shall not have any greater jurisdiction in relation to the laws and regulation relating to Her Majesty's Navy at sea, or under any Act providing for the discipline of Her Majesty's Navy, than may be from time to time conferred on such Court by Order in Council.

(4) Where a Court in a British possession exercises in respect of matters arising outside the body of a country or other like part of a British possession any jurisdiction exercisable under this Act, that jurisdiction shall be deemed to be exercised under this Act and not otherwise.

3. The legislature of a British possession may by any Colonial law

Power of Colonial legislature as to Admiralty jurisdiction.

(a) declare any Court of unlimited civil jurisdiction, whether original or appelate, in that possession to be a Colonial Court of Admiralty, and provide for the exercise by such Court of its jurisdiction under this Act, and limit territorially, or otherwise, the extent o such jurisdiction; and

(b) confer upon any inferior or subordinate court in that possession such partial or limited Admiralty jurisdiction under such regulations and with such appeal (if any) as may seem fit:

Provided that any such Colonial law shall not confer any jurisdiction which is not by this Act conferred upon a Colonial Court of Admiralty.

ation

her

's

e,ei

idin

the

kal

ris

a

colonial law for Her Majesty's assent.

jurisdiction of or practice or procedure in any Court of such possession in respect of the jurisdiction conferred by this Act, or alters any such Colonial law as above in this section mentioned, which has been previously passed, shall, unless previously approved by Her Majesty through a Secretary of State, either be reserved for the signification of Her Majesty's pleasure thereon, or contain a suspending clause providing that such law shall not come into operation until Her Majesty's pleasure thereon has been publicly signified in the British possession in which it has been passed.

Local Admiralty appeal.

5. Subject to rules of court under this Act, judgments of a court in a British possession given or made in the exercise of the jurisdiction conferred on it by this Act, shall be subject to the like local appeal, if any, as judgments of the court in the exercise of its ordinary civil jurisdiction, and the court having cognizance of such appeal shall for the purpose thereof possess all the jurisdiction by this Act conferred upon a Colonial Court of Admiralty.

Admiralty appeal to the Queen in Council.

6.-(1) The appeal from a judgment of any court in a British possession in the exercise of the jurisdiction conferred by this Act, either where there is as of right no local appeal or after a decision on local appeal, lies to Her Majesty the Queen in Council.

(2) Save as may be otherwise specially allowed in a particular case by Her Majesty the Queen in Council, an appeal under this section shall not be allowed-

(a) from any judgment not having the effect of a definite judgment unless the court appealed from has given leave for such appeal, nor

(b) fromany judgment unless the petition of appeal has been lodged within the time prescribed by rules, or if no time is prescribed within six months from the date of the judgment appealed against, or if leave to appeal has been given then from the date of such leave.

(3) For the purpose of appeals under this Act, Her Majesty the Queen in Council and the Judicial Committee of the Privy Council shall, subject to rules under this

section, have all such powers for making and enforcing judgments, whether interlocutory or final, for punishing contempts, for requiring the payment of money into court, or for any other purpose, as may be necessary, or as were possessed by the High Court of Delegates before the passing of the Act transferring the powers of such court to Her Majesty in Council, or as are for the time being possessed by the High Court in England or by the court appealed from in relation to the like matters as those forming the subject of appeals under this Act.

(4.) All Orders of the Queen in Council or the Judicial Committee of the Privy Council for the purposes aforesaid or otherwise in relation to appeals under this Act shall have full effect throughout Her Majesty's dominions, and in all places where Her Majesty has jurisdiction.

(5.) This section shall be in addition to and not in derogation of the authority of Her Majesty in Council or the Judicial Committee of the Privy Council arising otherwise than under this Act, and all enactments relating to appeals to Her Majesty in Council or to the

powers of Her Majesty in Council or the Judicial Committee of the Privy Council in relation to these appeals, whether for making rules and orders or otherwise, shall extend, save as otherwise directed by Her Majesty in Council, to appeals to Her Majesty in Council under this Act.

Rules of Court.

7.- (1.) Rules of court for regulating the procedure and practice (including fees and costs) in a court in a British possession in the exercise of the jurisdiction conferred by this Act, whether original or appellate, may be made by the same authority and in the same manner as rules touching the practice, procedure, fees, and costs in the said court in the exercise of its ordinary civil jurisdiction respectively are made:

Provided that the rules under this section shall not, save as provided by this Act, extend to matters relating to the slave trade, and shall not (save as provided by this section) come into operation until they have been approved by Her Majesty in Council, but on coming into operation shall have full effect as if enacted in this Act, and any enactment inconsistent therewith shall, so far as it is be

onsistent, be repealed.

2) It shall be lawful for Her Majesty in Council, in proving rules made under this section, to declare that rules so made with respect to any matters which pear to Her Majesty to be matters of detail or of local ncern may be revoked, varied or added to without the pproval required by this section.

(3) Such rules may provide for the exercise of any urisdiction conferred by this Act by the full court, or y any judge or judges thereof, and subject to any rules, here the ordinary civil jurisdiction of the court can in any case be exercised by a single judge, any jurisdiction onferred by this act may in the like case be exercised y a single judge.

Droits of Admiralty & of the Crown

---(1) Subject to the provisions of this section nothing n this act shall alter the application of any droits of dmiralty or droits of or forfeitures to the Crown in a British possession ; and such droits and forfeitures, hen condemned by a court of a British Possession in the exercise of the jurisdiction conferred by this Act , shall save as is otherwise provided by any other Act, be notifi-ed, accounted for, and dealt with in such manner as the Treasury from time to time direct and the officers of

every Colonial Court of Admiralty and of every other court in a British possession exercising Admiralty jurisdiction shall obey such directions in respect of the said droits and forfeitures as may be from time to time given by the Treasury.

(2) It shall be lawful for Her Majesty the Queen in Council by Order to direct that, subject to any conditions, exceptions, reservations, and regulations contained in the Order, the said droits and forfeitur condemned by a Court in a British possession shall form part of the revenues of that possession either for ever or for such limited term or subject to such revocation as may be specified in the Order.

(3) If and so long as any of such droits or forfeitures by virtue of this or any other Act form part of the revenues of the said possession the same shall subject to the provisions of any law for the time being applicable thereto, be notified, accounted for, and dealt with in manner directed by the Government of the possession, and the Treasury shall not have any power in relation thereto.

9.- (1) It shall be lawful for Her Majesty, by commission under the Great Seal, to empower the Admiralty to establish in a British possession any Vice Admiralty Court or Courts.

Power to establish Vice-Admiralty Court.

(2) Upon the establishment of a Vice-Admiralty Court in a British possession, the Admiralty, by writing under their hands and the seal of the office of Admiralty, in such form as the Admiralty direct, may appoint a judge, registrar, marshall, and other office of the court, and may cancel any such appointment; and in addition to any other jurisdiction of such court, may (subject to the limits imposed by this Act or the said commission from Her Majesty) vest in such court the whole or any part of the jurisdiction by or by virtue of this Act conferred upon any Courts of that British possession, and may vary or revoke such vesting, and while such vesting is in force the power of such last-mentioned courts toexercise the jurisdiction so vested shall be suspended.

Provided that-

(a) nothing in this section shall authorise a Vice-

Admiralty Court so established in India or in any British possession having a representative legislature, to exercise any jurisdiction, except for some purpose relating to prize, to Her Majesty's navy, to the slave trade, to the matters dealt with by the Foreign Enlistment Act, 1870, or the Pacific Islanders Protection Acts, 1872 and 1875, or to matters in which questions arise relating to treaties or conventions with foreign countries, or to international law; and

33 & 34 Vict. c. 90.
35 & 36 Vict. c. 19.
38 & 39 Vict. c. 51.

(b) in the event of a vacancy in the office of judge, registrar, marshall, or other officer of any Vice-Admiralty Court in a British possession, the Governor of that possession may appoint a fit person to fill the vacancy until an appointment to the office is made by the Admiralty.

(3) The provisions of this Act with respect to appeals to Her Majesty in Council from Courts in British possessions in the exercise of the jurisdiction conferred by this Act shall apply to appeals from Vice-Admiralty Courts, but the rules and orders made in relation to appeals from Vice Admiralty Courts may differ from the Rules made in relation to appeals from the said courts in British possessions.

(4) If Her Majesty at any time by commission under the Great Seal so directs, the Admiralty shall by writing under their hands and the seal of the office of Admiralty abolish a Vice-Admiralty Court established in any British possession under this section, and upon such abolition the jurisdiction of any Colonial Court of Admiralty in that possession which was previously suspended shall be revived.

Power to appoint a vice-admiral.

10. Nothing in this Act shall affect any power of appointing a vice-admiral in and for any British possession or any place therein; and whenever there is not a formally appointed vice-admiral in a British possession or any place therein, the Governor of the possession shall be ex-officio vice-admiral thereof.

Exception of Channel islands and other possessions.

11.-(1) The provisions of this Act with respect to Colonial Courts of Admiralty shall not apply to the Channel Islands.

(2) It shall be lawful for the Queen in Council by Order to declare, with respect to any

British possession which has not a represntative legislature, that the jurisdiction conferred by this Act on Colonial Courts of Admiralty shall not be vested in any court of such possession, or shall be vested only to the partial or limited extent specified in the Order.

Application of Act to Courts under Foreggn Jurisdiction Acts.

12. It shall be lawful for Her Majesty the Queen in Council by Orde to direct that this Act shall, subject to the conditions, exceptior and qualifications (if any) containe in the Order, apply to any Court established by Her Majesty for the exercise of jurisdiction in any place out of Her Majesty's dominions which is named in the Order as if that Court were a Colonial Court of Admiralty, and to provide for carrying into effect such application.

Rules for procedure in slave trade matters.

36 & 37 Vict. c. 59.
42 & 43 Vict. c. 38.

13.- (1) It shall be lawful for Her Majesty the Queen in Council by Order to make rules as to the practice and procedure (including fees and costs) to be observed in and the returns to be made from Colonial Courts of Admiralty and Vice-Admiralty Courts in the exercise of their jurisdiction in matters relating to the slave trade, and in and from East African Courts as defined by the Slave Trade (East African Courts) Acts, 1873 and 1879.

(2) Except when inconsistent with such Order in Council, the rules of Court for the time being in forc in a Colonail Court of Admiralty or Vice-Admiralty Court shall, so far as applicable, extend to proceedings in such court in matters relating to the slave trade.

(3) The provisions of this Act with respect to appeal to Her Majesty in Council, from Courts in British possessions in the exercise of the jurisdiction conferred by this Act, shall apply, with the necessary modofications, to appeals from judgments of any East African Court made or purporting to be made in exercise of the jurisdiction under the Slave Trade (East African Courts) Acts, 1873 and 1879.

Orders in Council.

14. It shall be lawful for Her Majesty in Council from time to time to make orde for the purposes authorised by this Act,

and to revoke and vary such Orders, and every such Order while in operation shall have effect as if it were part of this Act.

Interpretation. 15. In the construction of this Act, unless the context otherwise requires,-

The expression "representative legislature" means, in relation to a British possession, a legislature comprising a legislative body of which at least one half are elected by inhabitants of the British possession.

The expression "unlimited civil jurisdiction" means civil jurisdiction unlimited as to the value of the subject-matter at issue, or as to the amount that may be claimed or recovered.

The expression "judgment" includes a decree, order, and sentence.

The expression "appeal" means any appeal, rehearing, or review; and the expression "Local appeal" means an appeal to any court inferior to her Majesty in Council

The expression "Colonial law" means any Act, ordinance or other law having the force of legislative enactment in a British possession and made by any authority, other than the Imperial Parliament or Her Majesty in Council, competent to make laws for such possession.

Commencement of Act. 16.-(1) This Act shall, save as otherwise in this Act provided, come into force in every British possession on the first day of July one thousand eight hundred and ninety-one.

Provided that--

(a) This Act shall not come into force in any of the British possessions named in the First Schedule to this Act until Her Majesty so directs by Order in Council, and until the day named in that behalf in such Order; and

(b) If before any day above mentioned rules of court for the Colonial Court of Admiralty in any British possession have been approved by Her Majesty in Council, this Act may be proclaimed in that possession by the Governor thereof, and on such proclomation shall come into force on the day named in the proclomation.

(2) The day upon which this Act comes into force in any British possession shall, as regards that British

possession, be deemed to be the commencement of this Act.

26 & 27 Vict. c. 24.

(3) If, on the commencement of this Act in any British possession, rules of Court have not been approved by her Majesty in pursuance of this Act, the rules in force at such commencement under the Vice-Admiralty Courts Act, 1863, and in India the rules in force at such commencement regulating the respective Vice-Admiralty courts or Courts of Admiralty in India, including any rules made with reference to proceedings instituted on behalf of Her Majesty's ships, shall, so far as applicable, have effect in the Colonial Court or Courts of Admiralty of such possession, and in any Vice Admiralty Court established under this Act in that possession, as rules of court under this Act, and may be revoked and varied accordingly; and all fees payable under such rules may be taken in such manner as the Colonial Court may direct, so however that the amount of each such fee shall so nearly as practicable be paid to the same officer or person who but for the passing of this Act would have been entitled to receive the same in respect of like business. So far as any such rules are inapplicable or do not extend, the rules of court for the exercise by a court of its ordinary civil jurisdiction shall have effect as rules for the exercise ~~by the same~~ court of the jurisdiction conferred by this Act.

(4) At any time after the passing of this Act any Colonial law may be passed, and any Vice Admiralty Court may be established and jurisdiction vested in such Court, but any such law, establishment, or vesting shall not come into effect until the commencement of this Act.

Abolition of Vice Admiralty Courts.

17. On the commencement of this Act in any British possession, but subject to the provisions of this Act, every Vice-Admiralty Court in that possession shall be abolished; subject as follows,--

(1) All judgments of such Vice-Admiralty Court shall be executed and may be appealed from in like manner as if this Act had not passed, and all appeals from any Vice-Admiralty Court pending at the commencement of this Act shall be heard and determined, and the judgment thereon executed as nearly as may be in like manner as if this Act had not passed;

(2) All proceedings pending in the Vice-Admiralty Court in any British possession at the commencement of

this Act shall, notwithstanding the repeal of any enactment by this Act, be continued in a Colonial Court of Admiralty of the possession in manner directed by rules of court, and, so far as no such rule extends, in like manner, as nearly as may be, as if they had been originally begun in such court:

(3) Where any person holding an office, whether that of judge, registrar, or marshall, or any other office in any such Vice-Admiralty Court in a British possession, suffers any pecuniary loss in consequence of the abolition of such court, the Government of the British possession, on complaint of such person, shall provide that such person shall receive reasonable compensation (by way of an increase of salary or a capital sum, or otherwise) in respect of his loss, subject nevertheless to the performance, if required by the said Government, of the like duties as before such abolition:

(4) All books, papers, documents, office furniture, and other things at the commencement of this Act belonging, or appertaining to any Vice-Admiralty Court, shall be delivered over to the proper officer of the Colonial Court of Admiralty or be otherwise dealt with in such manner as, subject to any directions from Her Majesty the Governor may direct:

(5) Where, at the commencement of this Act in a British possession, any person holds a commission to act as advocate in any Vice Admiralty Court, abolished by this Act, either for Her Majesty or for the Admiralty, such commission shall be of the same avail in every court of the same British possession exercising jurisdiction under this Act, as if such court were the court mentioned or referred to in such commission.

18. The Acts specified in the Second Schedule to this Act shall, to the extent mentioned in the third column of that schedule, be repealed as respects any British possession as from the commencement of this Act in that possession, and as respects any courts out of Her Majesty's dominions as from the date of any Order applying this Act:

Repeal

Provided that-

(a) Any appeal against a judgment made before the commencement of this Act may be brought and any such appeal and any proceedings or appeals pending at the commencement of this Act may be carried on and

completed and carried into effect as if such repeal had not been enacted; and

(b) All enactments and rules at the passing of this Act in force touching the practice, procedure, fees, costs, and returns in matters relating to the slave trade in Vice-Admiralty courts and in East African courts shall have effect as rules made in pursuance of this Act, and shall apply to Colonial Courts of Admiralty, and may be altered and revoked accordingly.

-------oOo-------

S C H E D U L E S .

FIRST SCHEDULE.

Section 16. British Possessions in which Operation of Act is delayed.

New South Wales.
Victoria.
St. Helena.
British Honduras.

SECOND SCHEDULE.

Section 18.

Enactments Repealed.

Session and Chapter.	Title of Act.	Extent of Repeal.
56 Geo. 3. c.82.	An Act to render valid the judicial Acts of Surrogates of Vice-Admiralty Courts abroad, during vacancies in office of Judges of such courts.	The whole Act.
2 & 3 Will.4 c. 51.	An Act to regulate the practice and the fees in the Vice-Admiralty Courts abroad, and to obviate doubts as to their jurisdiction.	The whole Act
3 & 4 Will.4 c.41.	An Act for the better administration of justice in His Majesty's Privy Council .	Section two.
6 & 7 Vict.c.38.	An Act to make further regulations for facilitating the hearing appeals and other matters	In section two the words "or from any "Admiralty or "Vice-Admiralty

Session and Chapter.	Title of Act.	Extent of Repeal.
	by the Judicial Committee of the Privy Council.	"Court," and the words "or the "Lords Commissioners of Appeals in "prize causes or "their surrogates" In sevtion three the words "and the "High Court of "Admiralty of England," and the words "and from any Admiralty or Vice-Admiralty Court". In section five, from the first "the High Court of "Admiralty" to the end of the section In section seven, the words "and "from Admiralty or Vice-Admiralty "Courts". Sections nine and ten, so far as relates to maritime c auses.
6 & 7 Vict.c.38.-contd.		In section twelve, the words "or "maritime". In section fifteen the words "and Admiralty and "Vice-Admiralty"..
7 & 8 Vict.c.69.	An Act for amending an Act passed in the fourth year of the reign of his late Majesty, intituled, "An Act	In section twelve, the words "and from Admir-"alty and Vice-"Admiralty Courts" and so much of

Session and Chapter.	Title of Act.	Extent of Repeal.
7 & 8 Vict. c/69. contd.	for the better administration of "Justice in His "Majesty's Privy "Council," and to extend its jurisdiction and powers.	the rest of the section as relates to maritime causes.
26 Vict.c.24.	The Vice-Admiralty Courts Act, 1863.	The whole Act.
30 & 31 Vict.c.45.	The Vice-Admiralty Courts Act, 1867.	The whole Act.
36 & 37 Vict.c.59.	The Slave Trade (East African Courts) Act, 1873.	Sections four and five.
36 & 37 Vict.c.88.	The Slave Trade Act, 1873.	Section twenty as far as relates to the taxation of any costs, charge and expenses which can be taxed in pursuance of this Act. In section twenty-three the words "under the "Vice Admiralty "Courts Act, 1863."
38 &39 Vict.c.51.	The Pacific Islanders Protection Act, 1875.	So much of section six as authorises Her Majesty to confer Admiralty jurisdiction on any court.